WORLD IN
THEIR HANDS

WORLD IN THEIR HANDS

ORIGINAL THINKERS, DOERS, FIGHTERS, AND THE FUTURE OF CONSERVATION

STEVE JOHNSON

Guilford, Connecticut

An imprint of The Rowman & Littlefield Publishing Group, Inc.
4501 Forbes Blvd., Ste. 200
Lanham, MD 20706
www.rowman.com
Falcon and FalconGuides are registered trademarks and Make Adventure Your Story is a
trademark of The Rowman & Littlefield Publishing Group, Inc.

Distributed by NATIONAL BOOK NETWORK

British Library Cataloguing in Publication Information available

Library of Congress Cataloging-in-Publication Data

Names: Johnson, Steve, 1965- author.
Title: World in their hands : original thinkers, doers, fighters, and the future of
    conservation / Steve Johnson.
Description: Lanham, MD : The Rowman & Littlefield Publishing Group, Inc., [2021]
    | Summary: "World in their Hands tells the stories of those who saw the importance
    of our natural world and dedicated their lives to its conservation, preservation, and
    protection in diverse and inspiring ways"— Provided by publisher.
Identifiers: LCCN 2020053585 (print) | LCCN 2020053586 (ebook) | ISBN
    9781493057177 (hardcover) | ISBN 9781493057184 (epub)
Subjects: LCSH: Environmentalists—Biography. | Conservationists—Biography. |
    Environmentalism.
Classification: LCC GE55 .J65 2021 (print) | LCC GE55 (ebook) | DDC 333.72092/2
    [B]—dc23
LC record available at https://lccn.loc.gov/2020053585
LC ebook record available at https://lccn.loc.gov/2020053586

♾™ The paper used in this publication meets the minimum requirements of American
National Standard for Information Sciences—Permanence of Paper for Printed Library
Materials, ANSI/NISO Z39.48-1992.

Disclaimer: Quotations in this book, in offset text or otherwise, are attributed to the
persons profiled in each chapter.

For my kids
Jack and Lauren, you are my world

CONTENTS

CONTENTS

FOREWORD

GEORGE HAYDUKE WAS THE FIRST BADASS ENVIRONMENTAL superhero. A fictional character based on a real-life Vietnam vet, Hayduke was a beer-swilling, ex–Green Beret explosives expert who used vandalism, sabotage, and general mayhem to stop polluters and greedy corporations from despoiling the wilderness. "My job is to save the fucking wilderness. I don't know anything else worth saving," was Hayduke's credo.

Growing up, my heroes were either football players or action figures, definitely not environmentalists. Bo Jackson and GI Joe made great role models for a rough and tumble boy. I loved Nature and wanted to protect it, but there didn't seem to be a lot of environmentalists to choose from. Weren't ecologists all whiny tree-huggers screeching about spotted owls?

Then I read Edward Abbey's *The Monkey Wrench Gang* and discovered Hayduke. Here was a rugged outdoorsman, war veteran, and certifiable environmentalist action hero all rolled up into one. In fact, the fictional Monkey Wrench Gang, a crew of ecological hooligans, inspired the first group of legitimate environmental extremists, the direct-action organization, Earth First! Led by Dave Foreman, a Hayduke-esque character in his own right, Earth First! was a no-nonsense outfit that deployed eco-vandalism similar to that espoused in the novel. Their approach was militant and uncompromising. I was so drawn to Foreman's no-holds-barred environmentalism, my elementary school yearbook page quoted a phrase Foreman often cited: "Extremism in the defense of liberty is no vice."

Edward Abbey was just one of a cadre of the most important and influential voices in conservation, preservation, and environmental protection. The exploits, accomplishments, and philosophies of these distinguished environmental visionaries are described with eloquence in these pages. Long before being green became a trend, the luminaries herein made profound contributions to the way we think about Nature and man's relationship to the natural world. Today, their thoughtful reflections on the state of the planet and ways to save it have laid the groundwork for modern environmental activism, sustainability, and solution-seeking to the climate crisis. In their own way, the figures explored in this book were equally badass.

Steve Johnson breaks these historic figures into three categories: Thinkers, Doers, and Fighters. Though some are more well known than others, all faced adversity, political struggles, and even violence. Their stories are fascinating, and not just for an eco-geek with a library full of books by Nature writers.

Aldo Leopold, for example, was an author, philosopher, scientist, ecologist, forester, conservationist, and university professor. In his seminal environmental text, *A Sand County Almanac*, Leopold deployed his unique perspective to create a new conservation ethic. Leopold wanted to "decommodify" Nature and reimagine it as a community that includes man. "Conservation is the slow and laborious unfolding of a new relationship between people and land," he wrote. *A Sand County Almanac* sold more than two million copies, profoundly influencing the future environmental movement.

Unless you are a mountain climber in the American West, you may not be familiar with Bob Marshall, but he is no less influential than Leopold. As a forester, explorer, and conservationist in the 1930s, he described the preservation of undeveloped wilderness as one of the pressing issues of the day. "There is just one hope of repulsing the tyrannical ambition of civilization to conquer every niche on the whole earth. That hope is the organization of spirited people who will fight for the freedom of wilderness. . . . Just a few more years of hesitation and the only trace of that wilderness which has exerted such a fundamental influence in molding American character will lie in the musty pages of pioneer books." Marshall gave urgency to protecting wilderness. His explorations in wild lands, ability to describe their undiscovered treasures, and determination in preserving them led to the protection of over 5.4 million acres of American wilderness, including the Bob Marshall Wilderness Area in Montana.

World in Their Hands is loaded with tales of pioneering voices able to translate the complex and often disheartening condition of Nature and transform it into profound, positive change. The thinkers, doers, and fighters decipher the most fascinating creatures, landscapes, and Indigenous people on Earth and motivate governments, organizations, and ordinary citizens to save them. The book retells the compelling stories of over a dozen conservation pioneers in the hopes of imagining a more livable future.

World in Their Hands is a call to action. For over 20 years, I have dedicated my professional life to protecting the environment, owing a huge portion of my career to the environmental characters who inspired me, and many more like me, to act. Though no longer an extremist, my thinking has always been enriched by the different perspectives of diverse environmental thinkers. Faced with myriad pending ecological crises, ranging from climate change to disappearing biodiversity, this book comes at a profoundly important time in human history. Only by studying and learning from the lessons of our environmental forebearers, and dedication of the next generation, can we hope to avert a potential planetary crisis. Dive into this book and the world is in your hands, too.

—Jake Kheel, Vice President, Grupo Puntacana Foundation

BEGINNINGS

WE MET A BIRD NAMED RACHEL THAT DAY. MY KIDS WERE about 8 and 10 years old, swimming with the unfettered joy of youth in a northern Wisconsin lake when an enormous shadow drifted by. They looked up in time to see a bald eagle trace a crescent on a cobalt blue canvas and then dive steeply to the water. One second and a splash later, the eagle lifted off with a wiggling bass in its talons and two slow, effortless, wing flaps carried the bird to the top of an old white pine. Lunch ensued up there on a branch, and we had ringside seats to watch the rare event. The kids wanted to give the bird a name but couldn't think of one at first and then bickered when they did. But I had an idea.

"How about Rachel?"

They both looked at me funny. "Why Rachel? That doesn't seem like a good name for an eagle." I told them it was a perfect name and later that evening, showed them a book written by a famous lady named Rachel. After a brief history lesson, my kids understood that if it wasn't for that book, we probably wouldn't have seen the eagle in the tree that day.

Rachel Carson's *Silent Spring* is undeniably one of history's most iconic works of literature in its own right, as well as a pivotal moment in shaping the natural world we know today—and, indeed, the very identity of our nation, as the bald eagle is prominently displayed on America's official seals, flags, paper money and coins, stamps, and various departments of authority.

The eagle symbolizes freedom and strength, and Carson championed those qualities in painstaking studies of life in the sea in three gripping books prior to *Silent Spring*, which was, at the time, considered a handbook for the very future of all life on Earth. Indeed, Carson's chutzpah to call out mankind's presumed right to control Nature shaped the fiery and focused Pennsylvania native as one of the most prominent social revolutionaries we've known.

She was an ecologist before it was a thing and brought a vision and environmental ethic surrounding rising sea levels, melting glaciers, declining animal populations, and climate change long before all of these maladies were everyday news. Carson was the lightning rod for the modern environmental movement, and much of today's related research, study, processes, and mindset are made of her work.

Carson should be revered for her contributions to the natural world and modern society. Two young kids at a Wisconsin lake didn't know that, but they got to name a bald eagle Rachel and that was a special day.

HERE'S YOUR WORLD, DON'T SCREW IT UP

April of 2020 marked the fiftieth anniversary of Earth Day, the venerable global celebration promoting responsible stewardship of our planet's exquisite natural resources. This is a book about people with that same vision, who realized the importance of our natural world and dedicated their lives to conservation, preservation, and protection in diverse and inspiring ways: thinkers, doers, and fighters with environmental mojo decades prior to it being fashionable. Joining Ms. Carson in this book is a celebrity list of environmental luminaries with prescience, tireless devotion, bullheadedness, and profound musings that, even left in their own stimulating light, are to be celebrated and their names shouted from the mountaintops. This group made such an impact that their work and philosophies are still utilized or praised in today's natural world.

Perhaps the term *thinkers* conjures images of someone ensconced in a mahogany-paneled library, sitting in an old, musty high-back chair with pipe and journal in hand. That may indeed be the case in some walks of life, but mulling things over also extends beyond walls. Climb to the summit of a storied peak, wander quiet woods in a neighborhood park, stretch out in a flowery meadow—it is here and places like it all o'er the land where everyday folks can reflect on life around them. I'm as "everyday" as they come: not a scholar, scientist, or extraordinarily cerebral, but not a day goes by when the outdoors around me, my Out There, doesn't infuse my soul with some kind of moment.

Deep thinkers Henry David Thoreau and Aldo Leopold penned their ideas in *Walden* and *A Sand County Almanac*, and those titles are ubiquitous in educational settings across the country. Their musings reach to the heart of any wanderlust soul or backpacker today worth their weight in sporks and moleskin. In Thoreau's *Walking*, for instance, regarded as one of America's great essays, Henry David expounds on the enriching capabilities of a simple walk, or better yet, a saunter. And he sauntered nearly every day, not able or willing to sit still: "I cannot stay in my chamber for a single day without acquiring some rust."

Thoreau spoke eloquently to the spirit of walking, as well, and that it is not enough to "walk a mile into the woods bodily, without getting there in spirit."

What business have I in the woods, if I am thinking of something out of the woods?

Leopold's mantra speaks to an equal respect for and protection of Nature. His conservation ethic valued protection of Nature *for* humans but also *from* humans. For instance, in *A Sand County Almanac*, his seminal book encouraging a "land ethic" between people and the land upon which they live, he writes of these two ideals in this excerpt from one of my favorite passages:

We abuse land because we regard it as a commodity belonging to us. When we see land as a commodity to which we belong, we may begin to use it with love and respect.

Echoing Leopold's opinion that we aren't in charge of Nature nor should we aspire to be, Edward Abbey spouted off (rightly so) with a take-no-bullshit attitude about conservation in the Desert Southwest and indeed all over the world and told us straight up in his writing that our environment is in trouble. He was a *doer* to the core and his work belongs on the same literal and figurative shelf as Thoreau, Leopold, and John Muir. Recent years have seen a resurgence of respect for his Carson-esque views, as well, that just because we have the power to "manage" the world doesn't give us the right to do so. Two passages from *Down the River*:

It is not enough to understand the natural world; the point is to preserve it. Let Being be.

The beauty and existence of the natural world should be sufficient justification in itself for saving it all.

Well said, Ed. Abbey (who pushed and occasionally crossed legal boundaries, but who's counting?) was part of a group who geared up and went out to study, learn, record, report, and otherwise inspire the rest of the world. Muir is widely hailed as the most legendary of doers, roaming all over championing for conservation and preservation. Leopold, Sigurd Olson, Marshall, and friends joined forces and inspired the Wilderness Act, paperwork which we all hold dear every time we walk into our favorite wilderness area. Will Steger vigorously explored the farthest reaches of the poles, driving teams of dogsleds to show us riveting, extraordinarily beautiful, and fragile places.

Shortly after their wedding, Margaret Murie and her husband, Olaus (thinker-doer hybrids), embarked on an 8-month-long expedition to study caribou in Alaska's rugged Brooks Range. The driven couple spearheaded conservation; we have incomparable lands like the Arctic National Wildlife Refuge (ANWR) to show for it. Bob Marshall regularly hiked 30 or 40 miles in a day (with a smile on his face all the while), helped launch the Wilderness Society, protected special places, and his work influenced the millions of acres of unspoiled land we enjoy today.

Fighters share much in common with doers, but these folks also got vocal, sometimes loudly, standing their ground in the face of staunch adversity in political arenas, facing down bullheaded loggers or developers, simply refusing to budge in their commitment to saving a species or coveted piece of land.

Consider Minnesota native Marjory Stoneman Douglas, who moved to Miami in her nascent years and quickly recognized the irreplaceable beauty and significance of the Everglades. Douglas's book *The Everglades: River of Grass* redefined a long-held (oblivious) perception of the Everglades as merely a swamp rather than a vibrant incubator of life. The book is, in fact, often compared to Carson's *Silent Spring* for its influence on the "place" of our environment. Douglas fought valiantly for her beloved Everglades to her final days.

And how about Martin Litton? The legendary Grand Canyon river runner's name is largely unknown to the general public, but Litton's uncompromising efforts were pivotal in protecting the Grand from a pair of enormous dams that would have wreaked all manner of travesty on one of Earth's most treasured natural wonders. Litton once wrote:

> *I never felt it did any good to be reasonable about anything in conservation, because what you give away will never come back—ever.*

Litton fought alongside Abbey (they looked like a pair of ornery, wilderness-borne brothers) and David Brower; and, in 2004, Litton rowed the entire length of the Grand Canyon at age 89, never losing the gleam in his eye for the place he loved best.

In the midst of my heady college days, I heard stories of growing up in Rocky Mountain National Park and the big floods and vintage Colorado from an affable chap who sported an Abbey-Brower-Litton vibe and graded my raggedy essays. He still has that gleam for Nature, too, and like many of us, that fierce fire will never dim.

A BLUEPRINT FOR LIFE

The rest of this book's cast of characters left their own unique mark on the natural world around us, and it is through their work we continue, as best we can, to maintain some semblance of cohesion and partnership with the place in which we live. It's a mess out there, but it's not like we didn't see it coming. Procrastination, ignorance, and dominance are no longer options if we hope to stem the tide.

In our favor are the distinguished names on these pages and like-minded, farsighted envoys like Terry Tempest Williams, Rick Bass, Barry Lopez, Bill McKibben, John McPhee, Wendell Berry, and Annie Dillard. This group has carried the mantle high from their preceding Nature-soused ancestors and is adeptly, with grace, wisdom, and encouragement, passing it again to the march of their younger peers.

These pages look at key areas of environmental concern that have pervaded our culture and society for generations, drastically affecting its appearance and behavior. Chapters ahead highlight actions taken by these environmental movers and shakers, from highly visible feats to regulatory influence to the philosophical. We'll learn how they persisted in a miasma of adversity, pushback, constant political struggles, and even violence. Some believers were, in fact, killed for standing up for the well-being of this selfless, resilient, and abundant planet. In light of its treatment, Earth is forgiving as well, but our round and rotating orb can only take so much.

Human beings occupy an ironic place in the modern world. We have to take from it to survive but must preserve it as well. That's a difficult ask, considering a biped population swarming unchecked, its rampant individualism undoing wilderness with every step. We've learned along the way, at great cost, the sensitivity of flora and fauna habitats to climatic fluctuations, exhibited in harsh reality today. In my own tiny place here, I see this in real time; my kids are part of a generation mired in constant dire news—anemic winters, the veritable disappearance of Arctic ice, catastrophic fires and floods, and entire ecosystems literally migrating.

Most alarming is the very substance that gives us life: water. Everything—every single thing—relies on water. When it's gone, life goes with it and, yet, we continue to plunge well shaft skewers into the earth like a pincushion. The frightening result is playing out right in front of us—enormous chunks of desert land in Arizona cracked and dropped several feet when its groundwater foundation depleted to nearly empty. The venerable, revered Colorado River, flowing from Rocky Mountain headwaters for more than six million years, no longer makes it to the sea. The river just dries out and stops (with occasional trickles of hope some years when a skinny rivulet finds its way through). Southern California's Salton Sea is a stagnant, lifeless garbage dump of agricultural runoff. Aquifers beneath our feet are being sucked dry in the eye blink span of our lifetimes and, if we don't take heed, a reckoning will come when nothing comes out of the tap at the kitchen sink. Maybe then we'll understand. We are vulnerable but don't behave as such. We need to respect the whole of Nature for what it is, or realize an unsettling future.

As dim as the current landscape may sometimes seem, however, hope has a way about it. This book shares the results of dedicated efforts, including the founding of the National Park Service and the Wilderness Society, establishment of the Wilderness Act, and preservation of untold millions of acres of land. Inspired by the stories of history's conservation crusaders, we are buoyed by those who have picked up the torch in the 21st century, a renascence of Nature's confidantes and heralds of a call to arms for everyone to make the world a better place.

We are at a tipping point—well past it in many areas—and it is long past time to cease taking so much. Nothing else matters if we don't have a home. But a few ticks of time remain, perhaps, for the world to breathe a little, if we lend a hand.

I am humbled by the never-give-up tenacity of the names in this book, invigorated by what they stand for, and honored to share their stories with you.

THINKERS

One swallow does not make a summer, but one skein of geese, cleaving the murk of March thaw, is the Spring.

—ALDO LEOPOLD

WHEN I FIRST CONJURED THE THINKER/DOER/FIGHTER IDEA FOR this book, my initial image of thinkers was one likely similar to your own: an introspective soul gazing over, say, an emerald green alpine valley or craggy coastline fringed with frothy surf, or, perhaps, a wise old sage squirreled away in a dimly lit study. These are the Thoreaus and Leopolds and Muries, with deeply rooted views and a very cerebral attachment to Nature.

Where did this encompassing and genuine fondness take hold? Was it something in their DNA, a natural predisposition for the indispensable solitude of a pond in the woods or wild Alaska mountains? Perhaps it was what Thoreau called contact with Nature—a walk in the woods, a backyard garden, a snowy summit. Whatever the origin for the Thinkers, it sparked intermittent moments of inspiration, an afternoon of championing for conservation, or long months of penning journals and books.

When all was said and done, did those endless hours of thinking have an impact in the grand scheme? In a word, yes, and the results came to us in stages. In their time, the names in this book at the very least gave the rest of America pause to take a moment and think about the significance of the natural world. Today, we appreciate their work in the form of revered quotes, legendary tomes on various states of our natural world, and efforts that forever changed the physical and visceral landscape. Indeed, the very fact we are reading about them here and in dozens of other books is testament enough—but it goes far beyond ink on pages.

Thinkers share a collective concern for and attachment to this place that gives us life, from terra firma to skies above. He doesn't appear in this book, but consider this rumination from Shakespeare:

And this, our life exempt from public haunt, finds tongues in trees, books in running brooks, sermons in stones, and good in everything. One touch of nature makes the whole world kin.

One touch of Nature. The power in that one touch is beyond any manner of superlatives, but it is there in all of us. I was fortunate to grow up on the veranda of forests and lakes and a who's who of wild critters, but even a child of the city at some point feels the shade of a leafy tree or sees a bird land among its branches. From there, it's all what we make of it. But, regardless of how frequently or where we interact with it, Nature is with us all the while.

Perhaps for you it began with a haphazard crayon drawing of a tree and a squirrel on the grass below. Years later, maybe you hiked into a sprawling wilderness area or ambled through a city park or sat quietly and watched chickadees land on the feeder.

In one of those places or all of them, you found a moment and you became a thinker. Of things profound or simple is of no matter; what does is that you allowed Nature in to influence your view of what's Out There. And what's out there is a special, loving, giving, irreplaceable gift.

This is the perfect time, then, to introduce some of history's most influential thinkers, who stirred the embers in their day and left lasting legacies that continue to inspire and lead. Their words hold wisdom and promise—we just need to listen.

HENRY DAVID THOREAU

1817–1862

© GEO F. PARLOW

I went to the woods because I wished to live deliberately, to front only the essential facts of life, and see if I could not learn what it had to teach, and not, when I came to die, discover that I had not lived.

ARGUABLY, THIS IS ONE OF THOREAU'S MOST ICONIC AND INSPIRA-tional quotes. How many of us live deliberately, genuinely listening and learning, especially from Nature's voice? Thoreau was as deliberate as they come, making a decision near the midpoint of his short life to spend some quality time connecting closely with

Nature. In early spring of 1845, he packed meager belongings, borrowed an ax, and walked out of his hometown of Concord, Massachusetts, to build a small cabin on the shore of Walden Pond, a cozy locale only a short distance from town. He went there with an uncomplicated plan to experiment with a simpler life and, in doing so, created *Walden*, among literature's most influential works that endures today in its teachings and legacy. Indeed, you're doing all right when the likes of Gandhi and Martin Luther King Jr. name you as inspiration.

Henry David Thoreau was born, raised, and died in Concord. Before his transcendence to renowned conservation thinker and scribe, however, he carried a reputation as a Nature-loving nonconformist, favoring the idea of working Sundays and taking the other six days off (hear! hear!), instead of the other way around. He wasn't especially neighborly or all that concerned about personal hygiene, but he eventually found the focus to study in Harvard's hallowed halls, balancing a diverse course load that included the classics, philosophy, rhetoric, science, and mathematics. A year after graduating, he landed a job teaching in Concord, a tenure lasting only two weeks, after a clash with the dean over the idea of flogging unruly students.

Abruptly out of work, Henry went to work making pencils. His father owned a pencil factory housed in a mélange of sheds right behind the family home, where the Thoreau brood laboriously manufactured this most basic of writing tools. Interestingly, it was Henry David's tenacious mind that made the John Thoreau & Co. pencils the best in the country.

At the time, Europeans made far superior pencils, but Thoreau dove headlong into studying all there was to know about French and German pencils and invented an even better production process, catapulting his father's company to pencil prominence. Upon checking off that milestone, Henry David left the factory and started an elementary school with his brother, John. The school chapter of their lives was short-lived, however, as they had to close its doors when John became very ill and soon passed.

Interestingly, earlier in his life, Henry had met Ralph Waldo Emerson, who at the time had become a virtual divining rod of the Transcendentalist Era, a young and virile climate of liberal intellectualism. (Emerson, in fact, presented Harvard's commencement address the year Thoreau completed his studies, and they lived not far from each other in Concord.) Transcendentalists (including literary luminaries such as Margaret Fuller, Amos Alcott, and Walt Whitman) believed in a philosophical balance of respect for Nature, self-sufficiency, optimism, and the freedom—a veritable shove from the world—to go ahead and try new things. Emerson led the way by eloquently speaking to audiences far and wide on man's capacity to fully "know" Nature and, indeed, see the universe as something to get out and experience, rather than hold at arm's length as some kind of mysterious element.

He says as much in this simple statement on the influence of a forest: "In the woods, we return to reason and faith." There you have it; go walk in the woods to flee your daily habits and tendency to cling to normalcy. While Emerson initially took Thoreau under his wing, Henry David soon nurtured his own distinctive ideas and commitment to Nature far more intensely than Emerson's.

This became the driving force that cemented Thoreau's place as one of our time's most distinctive voices. Eventually, Thoreau took leave of his fellow philosophers and retreated to a small piece of land that Emerson owned on the shore of Walden Pond. Thoreau bought an old chicken coop and harvested its lumber, hauled the boards and accompanying building supplies to the pond, and built a little house. While the location was cozy and quiet, it was only a couple of miles from town, walking distance which he traveled frequently, as did a relatively regular (too regular, if you ask Henry) stream of visitors.

But nothing detracted from Thoreau's intentions of living at Walden Pond. Coinciding with his "economic experiment"

SONG OF THE THRUSH

Thoreau's beloved wood thrush lives throughout the eastern United States, although it trends to the reclusive. Instead of mimicking a challenger's call, males buck songbird trends by answering with a different tune. Numbers are declining due in large part to fragmented habitat and loss of adequate food sources. Cowbirds are trouble, as well, populating nearly every thrush nest with at least one of their own eggs.

of living via the one day on, six off scheme, he set about writing *A Week on the Concord and Merrimack Rivers* in tribute to his brother, John. The relative serenity at Walden Pond further fueled Henry's muse, which he channeled into *Walden*, a memoir/spiritual reflection hybrid on living simply. Indeed, his self-imposed isolation was a testament to how easy it is to live modestly if one can only see and appreciate the value in Nature and its inherent generosity of spirit. When Thoreau finally extracted himself from his two-year field trip, he proclaimed that life's so-called luxuries are "not only dispensable, but positive hindrances to the elevation of mankind. Man is rich in proportion to the number of things he can do without."

Coinciding with an awakening to Nature, he made no qualms of sharing thoughts on the finer things found outside—"the nonchalance of the butterfly carrying accident and change painted in a thousand hues upon its wings." A powerful message of an everyday performance related in a handful of words, and Thoreau's essays continued to reveal his argument that genuine *experience* with Nature can inspire a new and useful wisdom for life's other components. His prose was nothing short of artistic; he is widely viewed as the catalyst thrusting Nature writing into respectable literature, and indeed of Nature itself as a return to innocence and retreat to an essence of freedom.

I can attest to Nature's essence of freedom, its solace, inspiration, challenge, and lessons. Walking, living, touching, and seeing the natural world is the foundation upon which my life, my soul, were built and I don't let a day escape without contact with a sunbeam or raindrop, unruly wind or scent of a season. Speaking of contact, I first read Thoreau's homage to such sitting in a periphery seat of a college writing course. The moment didn't change my life in some enlightened manner heralded by angelic song, but it brought to the fore a mantra that galvanizes my days and will continue to the last of them. From *The Maine Woods*:

Talk of mysteries! Think of our life in nature,—daily to be shown matter, to come in contact with it,—rocks, trees, wind on our cheeks! the solid earth! the actual world! the common sense! Contact! Contact! Who are we? where are we?

It can take but a single touch; the point is to let it happen or reach to it with intent. For example, I relate in robust spirit to Thoreau's appreciation of the common wood thrush, an energetic and melodious little bird that makes many appearances in his writing. He likened the thrush as the herald of all that is right with the wild: "The thrush alone declares the immortal wealth and vigor that is in the forest." In his journals, he bestows high honor upon the thrush, and there has likely never been a more eloquent description of its melody:

. . . this bird never fails to speak to me out of an ether purer than that I breathe, of immortal beauty and vigor. He deepens the significance of all things seen in the light of his strain. He sings to make men take higher and truer views of things.

Words like that were part and parcel to Thoreau's intensely personal and introspective relationship with Nature, one that set him apart from society's well-trodden road. This chorus of his voice came to light in a particularly poignant message in *Walking*, a lecture-turned-essay on the heartbeat of wildness and all that it brings to our everyday lives, even if it is merely a walk in the woods. "I believe that there is a subtle magnetism in Nature which, if we unconsciously yield to it, will direct us aright."

His deep passion clearly evident in his words, it is difficult not to be filled with an awakening of sorts, a realization that the spirit of wilderness is within us, not only a distant mysterious location on a dusty and wrinkled map. Never discount the power of a dusty, wrinkled map, however; I've followed the lead of many and discovered a new wilderness spirit every time.

Thoreau was on to something in this realm and nailed it in what is widely regarded as his most well-known quote, "in wildness is the preservation of the world," leading this passage from *Walking*:

> *The West of which I speak is but another name for the Wild; and what I have been preparing to say is, that in Wildness is the preservation of the world. Every tree sends its fibres forth in search of the Wild. The cities import it at any price. Men plough and sail for it. From the forest and wilderness come the tonics and barks which brace mankind.*

Is it so tenuous a wish that these words don't continue falling on deaf ears? In the time it took me to write this single page, another huge chunk of the Amazon, a place of tonics and barks and other irreplaceable gifts, was slashed and burned to oblivion. Surely, there is a Thoreau-esque wilderness ethos, a respect for life, pervasive in enough of us to find destruction of that magnitude unacceptable? Vision that sees a world beyond the meager years of our own lives?

Walking a pine forest or ocean shore or desert arroyo, it takes only the slightest meditative halt to feel, hear, smell, touch what is around you. Try it today, and tomorrow, too. It will make a difference. In autumn, go walk in the woods, breathe deep, and tell me that doesn't make you smile. Stand there awhile. Listen to the chickadees. Watch a bright orange maple leaf on a fast-twitch, zigzag descent; let it hit you in the cheek, glance off your arm, and land at your feet. You just saw the last chapter of a beautiful, moving, silent, life story. Wander a fall festival and drink apple cider and eat caramel apples, apple pie, and corn on the cob. The world is all reds and golds, frosty mornings and evening campfires. Let another leaf land.

And mull for a moment how our friend Henry David viewed that kind of a world. From his journals:

The earth I tread on is not a dead, inert mass. It is a body— has a spirit—is organic—and fluid to the influence of its spirit—and to whatever particle of that spirit is in me.

Organic indeed, as he goes on in a somewhat unappetizing yet alluring way to describe springtime when frost oozes from the ground: "If the weather is too warm and rainy or long continued it becomes mere diarrhea—mud and clay relaxed." He continues with thoughts on Earth's place as the start of all life in writing: "Nature has some bowels and there again she is mother of humanity . . . the globe is a worthier place for these creations. This slumbering life that may awake. Even the solid globe is permeated by the living law."

He ends the passage with an abrupt but appropriate refrain: "It is the most living of creatures. No doubt all creatures that live on its surface are but parasites."

Interestingly, few of Thoreau's contemporaries shared his increasing devotion to wilderness, Emerson among them. Henry David simply had his own ideas of and made his own experiences in Nature and then recorded it all in extensive journals. Indeed, his views on mankind's intrinsic connection to Nature diverged from most every other person in America, who were at the time all but reveling in murmurs of the country's rapidly approaching collision with the din of perceived industrial glory and riches.

Keep in mind that even Thoreau's glossy sheen was tinged with hypocrisy. As America's virgin wilderness vanished by the day, its people were, for lack of better words, duped into believing that the baubles of a grand new mechanized world would make up for the loss of wild places. While Thoreau never hesitated to voice his love of Nature, he made little effort to preserve it. In fact, he at one time worked as a surveyor plotting land for development and essentially sat back and watched the industrial world obliterate his once-idyllic hometown. Critics viewed Thoreau as blinded by his own optimism, more enraptured by a rosy future than concerned with matters unfolding in front of him, seduced by the belief that simply staying positive will guard against all that ails us.

A positive outlook is great to a point, unless we just sit on our hands. We must weave Nature's wonderful experiences and lessons back into our everyday world if we hope to slow society's destructive tide. And, so far, we've been ineffective at best on conservation fronts, as rampant pillaging of the planet's resources continues unabated.

Nevertheless, it is refreshing, even in hindsight, to know that our friend Thoreau appreciated the little things like being "refreshed by the flux of sparkling streams" and the nonchalance of the butterfly. He held minnows and bald eagles in equally high esteem and wrote with verve on natural and direct experiences with the whole of Nature, down to the finest of details.

Contact!

HIS LEGACY

Throughout the penning of enduring, influential work and all his other post-college endeavors, Thoreau battled tuberculosis. His symptoms devolved rapidly in 1859 and he passed at the far-too-young age of 44. Early mentor Emerson paid respects with these words, driving home Thoreau's enormous and lasting impact: "The country knows not yet, or in the least part, how great a son it has lost. His soul was made for the noblest society; he had in a short life exhausted the capabilities of this world; wherever there is knowledge, wherever there is virtue, wherever there is beauty, he will find a home."

Exhausted the capabilities of the world. An exquisite description of Thoreau's approach toward and accomplishments within his life and an enviable refrain. Imagine our potential if we seized every day by the scruff of the neck and reveled in everything it had to offer. It was that blend of the natural world and a "successful" life that inspired—and still does—everyone from spit-polished ecologists to anarchists (Thoreau sported a healthy rebellious streak of his own) to anyone with the capacity to welcome a new path of thinking. He was a fierce believer in refusing to let society dictate how people should work and live and gave no quarter in his views on mankind's ability to exist in harmony with Nature.

In the realm of the written word, Thoreau's legacy is reflected in the work of his immediate successors, John Muir and John Burroughs, as well as a parade of later environmental heavyweights—think Carson, Abbey, Dillard, Williams, McKibben, Quammen, Bass, and many more. Former president Barack Obama signed the proclamation establishing the Katahdin Woods and Waters National Monument; the Kennedy family lineage began in Concord and Thoreau's was prevalent throughout their reign. The list goes on, and even casual fans will notice the Thoreauvian sway, far beyond *Walden*, upon many of today's natural wonders and movements; in fact, his presence is arguably more prevalent in our time than his own.

Best of all, there's a bright-eyed kid in a classroom somewhere right now reading about contact with Nature and tapping into a spirit of living in step with all that is around us. We need that spirit today—Nature needs it.

Go out there and touch it.

ROBERT STERLING YARD

1861–1945

PHOTOGRAPH BY HARRIS & EWING

*I, the treader of dusty city streets, boldly claim common kin-
ship with you of the plains, the mountains, and the glaciers.*

YELLOWSTONE. THE NAME ALONE INVOKES IMAGES OF GEYSERS
and skyscraper waterfalls and hot springs. El Capitan, John
Muir, its own Grand Canyon. Yellowstone is also America's first
national park and, in fact, the first place on Earth known as a
"national park." A very quiet locale when bestowed its official park
status in 1872, Yellowstone today attracts in the neighborhood
of four million visitors every year. Perhaps you are one of them

and this is your favorite destination, or maybe wanderlust takes you to our country's other splendiferous national parks. You have sixty-two to choose from, made of various shapes and sizes and chock-full of hypnotically beautiful sights and sounds.

You can tip a cap to Robert Sterling Yard for making it all possible and, at the same time, be forgiven if his name doesn't ring a bell. In the pantheon of conservation movers and shakers, Yard held stage with Bob Marshall, Aldo Leopold, Harvey Broome, Benton MacKaye, Ernest Oberholzer, Bernard Frank, and Harold Anderson to form the Wilderness Society in 1935. But in the public's field of view at the time, and today's as well, Yard flew under the radar, leveraging the indelible power of the written word to drive home the importance of place and very substance of conservation. In the process he dug in his heels at the pointy end of our country's conservation movement and played a critical role in the establishment of the National Park Service.

Like his compatriot Bob Marshall, Yard was New York–born and –bred. Unlike Marshall, however, Yard was by no means a skilled outdoorsman or dogged explorer. Mr. Yard was a word guy, honing his Princeton-educated writing chops on the late 1800s reporter beat for the *New York Sun* and *New York Herald*. He went on to hold editor posts at the *Herald* and *The Century Magazine*, followed by a 15-year stint in the publishing industry when his longtime friend Stephen Mather came calling. The two first met while working for the *Sun*, and after making millions as a savvy businessman, Mather eventually migrated to Washington, DC, as assistant to the secretary of the interior. Conservation-minded at heart, Mather urged his friend to join him in efforts to educate the public and convey the need for and benefit of a new management agency for America's national parks. Still in their nascent years, the parks were wonderful places but not fully understood by society and saw relatively few visitors. Mather leveraged his position to establish Yard as the Department of the Interior's publicity chief in 1915, and that opened the conservation floodgates. Yard felt a keen connection to our natural world and dove headlong into promoting its tending with an approachable, eloquent way with words and tenacity to a goal.

"It is not necessary to become a geologist or a botanist or a zoologist to penetrate Nature's secrets, nor to tell schists from granites, classify the conifers or call a bird by its Latin name. A few popular books, many pictures carefully studied and a sincere desire will open the window upon an old world made new."

He blended existing data and pictures from other popular destinations Americans fancied at the time (think Switzerland, Germany, Italy, and Canada, to name a few) with a natural finesse to engage with people. In his first year in Washington, he compiled *The National Parks Portfolio*. Published the following year, this was a first of its kind assemblage of entertaining and educational narrative accompanied by riveting photos of America's scenic places. Yard wondered why his compatriots traveled around the world instead of visiting scenic spectacles in their own backyard: "Our national parks have had little patronage because few have ever heard of them." As such, the ultimate goal of his portfolio was promoting parks as tourist destinations in a way that generated interest from the American people and subsequently sparked an economic boost while conserving park lands and wilderness areas. He saw the parks as a (responsible) business proposition: "We have the biggest and finest stock of scenery in the world and there is an enormous market for it." He reinforced his views in further support of wild lands:

Unconnected with the Government and absolutely independent of political or other adverse influences, it has become the fearless and outspoken defender of the people's parks and the wildlife within them against the constant, and just now the very dangerous, assaults of commercial interests. Americans who have not yet visited the National Parks and may never visit them find keen pleasure in the photographs and paintings of these masterpieces of nature and in the written descriptions of their wonders.

Our National Parks, then, are the easy and fascinating charts to a comprehension which will remake this whole land of ours into a thing of supreme interest.

Working in tandem with Mather, Yard spread his parks portfolio from coast to coast. Nearly 300,000 prominent US residents, including every single member of Congress, received a copy in what became a wildly successful crusade in support of Nature. And Yard didn't stop there—his pen rarely rested as he scribed more than 1,000 related articles (in just a two-year period between 1917 and 1919) for publications across the country, along with three of his most influential works—*The Top of the Continent, Glimpses of Our National Parks*, and *The Book of National Parks*—in efforts to lure the public to America's wild places and appreciate their importance. Yard presented consistent salvos supporting the formation of a managing agency for our parks; one in particular was as powerful as it was simple: "Stay with the wilderness and it will repay you a thousandfold." Words to live by, indeed.

Unsurprisingly, statements like that and the rest of his pro-lific writing captured the attention of Congress. In August of 1916, President Woodrow Wilson signed a bill establishing the National Park Service. Mather served as the organization's first director and Yard managed its educational division as well as serving as executive secretary. Yard continued to excel in commu-nicating the message of conservation of "American masterpieces."

While the United States was not entirely new to recognizing the presence and benefit of parks (fourteen parks and twenty-two monuments had been established from 1872 to Yard's work in

1915), the process was far from streamlined and lacked organized resource management. The new park service was heralded as panacea to that disarray and Yard spearheaded solutions with verve, including the designation of recreation within the parks part and parcel to their conservation.

"Our national parks system is a national museum. Its purpose is to preserve forever certain areas of extraordinary scenic magnificence in a condition of primitive nature. Its recreational value is also very great, but recreation is not distinctive of the system. The function which alone distinguishes the national parks is the museum function made possible only by the parks' complete conservation."

All was well and good until 1919, when Yard was forced to leave the NPS due to evidence of Mather inappropriately funding Yard's salary. Yard did not, however, go quietly into that good night. He had long held hope of a parks association of private citizens with dedicated concern for wild places and immediately funneled Mather's last payment to the creation of the National Parks Association (NPA), a citizens group advocating for public protection and support of the National Park Service. His efforts were a hit; the two groups went on to collaborate on many projects and issues, in a sort of "behind closed doors" approach free of federal politics. He also crafted a comprehensive education program to attract artists, writers, and students to the parks.

Yard settled into the NPA's executive secretary role, but it wasn't long before he and Mather, still with the Department of the Interior, butted heads over particular park policies and Yard's desire to retain our national parks' true wilderness integrity. Yard was fully behind responsible use of the parks but felt much of their lands should be left wild, the way we found them, not overrun with concession stands, roads carrying parades of

THE VOICE OF THE PARKS

America's treasured national parks have some heavyweight support protecting their flanks in the National Parks Conservation Association. More than one million members strong, the NPCA is "the voice of America's national parks," dedicated to preserving scenic jewels from Olympic to Voyageurs to the Virgin Islands. Now in their second century, the group continues to make great strides in drawing attention to our parks' critical issues including climate change, energy use, and resource stewardship.

automobiles, and hordes of people trampling all over Nature's showcase sights. He had no qualms in voicing concerns that some of the newly designated parks weren't up to what he viewed as "national park standards," while Mather and then–NPS assistant director Horace Albright welcomed more cars bringing more people. Mather in particular was not interested in wildlife protection in the parks, favored extermination of predators, and also supported luxe accommodations with all the comforts of home and copious entertainment options. This grated on Yard's values to the point of more than just workday spats.

Eventually, the impasse and Yard's stalwart commitment to preservation inspired his work in cofounding The Wilderness Society, where he parlayed his writing chops as the first editor and contemplator of *The Living Wilderness*, the group's flagship publication. He made an instant impact penning the society's creed:

> *The inherent rights of succeeding generations to study, enjoy and use fine examples of primeval America is a responsibility of this generation.*

Imagine what our world would look and feel like today if that mantra rooted as part of our culture and not just a passing thought. In addition to orchestrating powerful words, Yard took on a great deal of The Wilderness Society's daily tasks and infused unbounded energy in fostering conservation's critical message. Especially poignant was his passion for telling it like it was, with "warfare in Congress" that saved the national parks from enormous and unneeded water power projects like Glen Canyon and other boondoggles that eviscerated most of our other primitive lands. He brought to light the craze to "build all the highways possible everywhere while billions may yet be borrowed from the unlucky future . . . the fashion is to barber and manicure wild America."

Yard continued to campaign for conservation through a severe bout of pneumonia, compiling articles for *The Living Wilderness* and managing The Wilderness Society's work from his bed. However, while declining health slowed his pace, his dedication shined like the aurora; our parks and public lands today wouldn't be the same without him. Yard's Wilderness Society cofounder Ernest Oberholzer perhaps said it best when describing his colleague's "vitality of inspiration": "Few men in America have ever had such understanding of the spiritual quality of the American scene, and fewer still the voice to go with it."

HIS LEGACY

The parks are worth the effort: a six-word argument for putting in the work to save America's treasured places. Robert Yard backed it up with the kind of dedication to a cause that moved mountains—and kept them in one piece. His words alone were impetus for public and federal movements that ultimately conserved some of the most brilliant displays of scenic splendor on Earth. Step one foot into a national park anywhere in the country and raise a glass to Bob; it is thanks in large part to him that we have such places in which to hike, camp, ruminate, and breathe deeply of the very soul of where we live. Yard reflects on just a few beauteous destinations:

Rocky Mountain National Park

There is probably no other scenic neighborhood of the first order which combines mountain outlines so bold with a quality of beauty so intimate and refined. Just to live in the valleys in the eloquent and ever-changing presence of these carved and tinted peaks is itself satisfaction. But to climb into their embrace, to know them in the intimacy of their bare summits and their flowered, glaciated gorges, is to turn a new and unforgettable page in experience.

Scenic neighborhoods of the first order indeed, and the mountains' embrace is comfort unlike any other. To me, there is no purer elixir than the rarified air of an alpine peak, and peace found in the folds of its valleys.

Yellowstone

The fitting playground and pleasure resort of a great people; it is also the ideal summer school of nature study.

Crater Lake

A gem of wonderful color in a setting of pearly lavas relieved by patches of pine green and snow white.

Grand Canyon

Even the most superficial description of this enormous spectacle may not be put in words. The wanderer upon the rim overlooks a thousand square miles of pyramids and minarets carved from the painted depths. There is no measure, nothing which the eye can grasp, the mind fathom.

Yard was a generally cautious fellow and skirted confrontation unless it directly affected preservation. His prowess with communicating the importance of our natural places gave rise to the National Parks Conservation Association and National Park

Service, hosting nearly 400 individual regions made of more than eighty-four million acres. His enduring values carried on with his Wilderness Society colleagues as Howard Zahniser and Olaus Murie managed the organization over the 20 years following Yard's death, and Zahniser shepherded *The Living Wilderness* as one of America's most successful conservation publications. The Wilderness Society alone spearheaded the designation of more than one hundred million acres of land to the National Wilderness Preservation System.

Yard also solidified the Sierra Club as a powerful ally in preserving Nature and all manner of related activities, a relationship that played a critical role in passing the Wilderness Act in 1964 and protecting especially important natural areas, from national forests to wildlife refuges.

"We believe that the great majority of careless and casual enjoyers of the out-of-doors would join heartily in preservation if only he realized the exquisiteness of primeval nature, the majesty of much of it, and that once destroyed it can never be returned to its thrilling sequence from the infinite."

ALDO LEOPOLD

1887–1948

Like winds and sunsets, wild things were taken for granted until progress began to do away with them. Now we face the question whether a still higher "standard of living" is worth its cost in things natural, wild and free.

DUST BOWL DROUGHTS AND THE GREAT DEPRESSION WERE BUT temporary digressions. On a scouting trip for hunting land in 1935, Aldo Leopold came upon an abandoned, shabby farm near the junction of a pair of narrow, little-traveled sand roads in south central Wisconsin. Composed of 80 acres of scruffy land logged clean, overgrazed, and stomped into submission by cows and other livestock, curb appeal was not in great abundance. The place was frayed at the edges, barren in the middle aside from a raggedy old chicken coop and a marsh, and left to wither from neglect. But Leopold recognized a spirit in the stubble. Or maybe that's our romantic perception of it all; it could be he simply stumbled onto a good deal (eight dollars an acre!) for property and grabbed it.

That piece of scrub land adjacent to the Wisconsin River became a National Historic Landmark and inspiration to one of our country's most influential conservationists. Aldo Leopold was born and lived his nascent childhood years in his grandparents' sprawling Italianate mansion in Burlington, Iowa, perched atop a bluff overlooking the Mississippi River valley. Complementing splendid views, the wooded valley's hidden backwaters and trails with a backdrop of train whistles from the river bridge were the stuff of dreams for a young boy enchanted with Nature.

Leopold came from a long lineage of outdoors spirit and conservation ideals. His grandfather, Charles, was a force in Burlington and leveraged his naturalist chops to influence preservation of land for parks designed with native plants. He carried the same vision at home, with extensive transformation of worn and sullied land into a place of vibrant flora and a bluffside hiking trail.

Aldo's father was also keen for the outdoors, traveling through still-young midwestern landscapes selling farm and ranch wares. Carl Leopold passed on a curiosity and respect for Nature to his children (Aldo, Marie, and Carl Jr.) with frequent adventures in the woods and impromptu lessons about their surroundings. Aldo honed his landscaping and gardening chops, as well, and became skilled in tending to various plant species while simultaneously keeping eyes and ears open for birds. He was fascinated with native birds and never missed an opportunity to record their counts, species, and songs—a talent that would serve him (and, one day, us) well later in life.

Leopold took his penchant for steely-eyed observation and meticulous notetaking to Yale University in pursuit of a master's degree in forestry and never shied from revealing his conservationist side. I am especially intrigued by one of his predict-the-future-like remarks in a class project, where he announced concern for the state of forests: "Their destruction involves the overturning of Nature's balance, and gradually but inevitably changes in climate will follow." One look at forestland around the world today confirms his belief.

Graduation buzz had hardly settled before an eager Leopold accepted a position at the US Forest Service (USFS), still in its infancy and chock-full of opportunity to ascend the ranks. He scored his choice of field locations in New Mexico and dove headlong into work, making supervisor of Carson National Forest in just three years.

Leopold was never afraid to speak his mind with conviction and encouraged the USFS to manage their lands responsibly "according to the effects on the forest," not simply for resource use:

"To those devoid of imagination a blank place on the map is a useless waste; to others, the most valuable part."

He connected early to the idea of preserving already vanishing wildlife and their habitats for his children and theirs to come, an ethic that inspired diligent compilations of data on forest animal species' inherent value. From that data came a comprehensive guide to game and fish, a first for the Forest Service and the nation. He pleaded for species diversity and presented actionable ideas to make it happen, eventually inheriting the title of the "father of wildlife management and ecology."

Later, a quiet, peaceful Sunday morning fishing at the headwaters of the Gila River proved fortuitous for Leopold, and the rest of us. Something stirred inside Aldo that day—probably the enticing blend of birdsong, water pulsing with trout, air laced with the heady, addictive scent of pine, and good old-fashioned peace and quiet. A sweet elixir, indeed, and why shouldn't everyone have the opportunity to imbibe? According to Aldo, "Wilderness is the one kind of playground which mankind cannot build to order."

On that sentiment's note, a meeting with fellow forester Arthur Carhart sparked what became a wilderness preservation movement.

Carhart echoed Leopold's affinity for wild lands, recommending the Forest Service set aside Colorado's Trappers Lake as preserved wilderness. But the visionary pair faced a proverbial uphill battle—the Forest Service heretofore placed emphasis only on conserving lands suitable for future "management" or creating national parks laced with intruding roads that opened floodgates of tourists. Leopold didn't trust the National Park Service; management was lax at best and their reputation sullied by what Aldo viewed as misdirected and failed attempts at making "improvements" to the land.

Leopold spent a few years butting heads with various chief foresters while diving headlong into studying the devastating effects of overgrazing, overlogging, overuse—and overlooking. Forestland in Colorado and New Mexico had been beaten down and denuded of virtually all its original vigor. Leopold presented his findings on various stages and eventually earned reluctant kudos from his chief forester, who still grappled with Aldo's restless energy. Leopold was offered a transfer to the University of Wisconsin's Forest Products Laboratory. He initially declined, choosing instead to continue pushing for wilderness preservation and the mantra that logging, extraction, and other commercial forest use was not (and still isn't) always the best or only choice. He believed strongly in the inherent and palpable soul of the outdoors and never hesitated to state as much. "Only the mountain has lived long enough to listen objectively to the howl of a wolf."

Leopold drove his opinion home with an exhaustively researched and detailed proposal to preserve the Gila Forest's canyonlands as wilderness. While immediate supervisors and coworkers were duly impressed, the proposal sat idly on a desk while the Forest Service and US government continued fanning the flames of commercializing Nature. Aldo vehemently protested: "Recreational development is a job not of building roads into lovely country, but of building receptivity into the still unlovely human mind."

His proposal was voted down but his voice was heard and words read across the country. Leopold responded with poise and verve to all critics of the idea of wilderness preservation pervading public minds, bolstered with support from like-minded colleagues—Carhart, Bob Marshall, Ernest Oberholzer, Harvey Broome. I particularly enjoy Leopold's friend Frank Waugh's take: "When Leopold's trumpet call rang through the forest, echoes came back from every quarter." It turned out that millions of Americans shared the wilderness ideal and, through an unprecedented call to arms, Leopold's tireless work ushered in our country's most significant preservation moment.

He looked closer at the Wisconsin opportunity, decided the time was right for a change, and moved north. Only days after leaving his longtime post in New Mexico, the Forest Service approved Leopold's plan for the Gila Wilderness Area, America's first and impetus for the establishment of the Wilderness Act 40 years later. In fact, his thoughts on land use provided a foundation for the act and influenced its verbiage:

We abuse land because we regard it as a commodity belonging to us. When we see land as a community to which we belong, we may begin to use it with love and respect.

Leopold worked hard at his new forest lab position but studying and testing commercial products every day tested his limits; he longed to be out in the woods and jumped at any available forest inspection that brought him there. He also spent nearly every weekend with his family at their land in the country. One of their first projects was resurrecting the chicken coop to a habitable state. The floor was buried somewhere beneath a deep layer of aged manure, and siding boards listed at awkward angles or clutched desperately to a rusty nail or two. Nevertheless, the Leopolds turned the old coop into The Shack, a cozy little base camp for a life chapter primed to imprint indelible memories and, in true Aldo fashion, research and experiments that influenced conservation practices and inspired *A Sand County Almanac*, one of history's most influential works of Nature writing.

Undaunted by the land's untidy appearance, the Leopold family took to it with care and attention akin to raising a child. This was a place to restore Nature's ecological infirm and, with Aldo's guided hand, they embarked on an ambitious experiment: planting 50,000 pine trees, restoring prairies, and recording changes as the land bloomed with a new spirit.

Aldo, of course, reveled in the journaling of it all, and his extensive and meticulous notetaking was displayed in arguably no finer form than his curiosity and subsequent study of birdsong. He enjoyed the melodious lyrics of birds simply for their gentle peace but saw something more in their morning concertos. He believed that individual bird species sing their first notes at different degrees of morning light, supporting his hypothesis by spending untold hours outside the shack with a light meter and journal, recording times, relative brightness, frequency, and location of avian song. Keep in mind that Leopold didn't have a fancy recording device: just a trained ear, journal, and unflagging devotion. His work was so detailed and complete, in fact, that nearly 70 years later, researchers in the young field of soundscape ecology transformed Leopold's journal notes into an audio "retelling" of indigo buntings, red cardinals, grosbeaks, orioles, and a host of other choral members.

Building further on his already deep connection to Nature, time on his family's land played a big role in shaping Leopold's

WHAT OUGHT TO BE

One of the grandest displays of Aldo Leopold's vision and conservation ethic rings the south shore of Lake Wingra at the University of Wisconsin Arboretum. A dilapidated old farm became the unlikely incubator of ecological restoration, 1930s ecology's newest discipline. Mulling over plans to rebuild an arboretum, Leopold and the rest of the Arb committee diverted from the traditional path of importing ornamental trees, choosing instead to create an homage to Wisconsin's native flora and fauna, from prairies to marshes to pine forests. Restoration efforts continue; today, the UW Arboretum is one of America's most respected, boasting 1,200 acres of gardens and trails.

land ethic, a personal and closely held attraction and respect for his surroundings that would go on to shape a philosophy and formal area of study.

A land ethic changes the role of Homo sapiens from conqueror of the land-community to plain member and citizen of it. It implies respect for his fellow-members and also respect for the community as such.

Ethics at their core are based on all members of a particular community treating each other with respect for a unified mutual benefit. A land ethic broadens the scope to include Earth's other ingredients—soil, water, flora, and fauna—and Leopold believed in an interconnected relationship between people and the land which he shared not as a straight-laced definition but rather tangible values. He writes in *A Sand County Almanac*: "We can only be ethical in relation to something we can see, understand, feel, love or otherwise have faith in. Conservation is a state of harmony between men and land."

On the surface, a land ethic doesn't seem a complicated endeavor: wise use of our land and water resources with productive and responsible farming, forestry, and other land interaction that doesn't interfere with the natural way of things. Straightforward ideas but clearly difficult to grasp, incomprehensible apparently, for those who adhere to the far too prevalent human ideal of lording over instead of living with. Too often we forget (disregard) the fact that we live on and with a gracious planet allowing copious freedoms and endless tapestries of unimaginable beauty. You'd think it only natural to treat the place with a little respect, but we choose to take from it, extracting and diverting and digging, "improving" until the pristine is unrecognizable, eradicating entire species of magnificent animals and plants, and removing their right—the same one we claim to have—to continue living here.

All ethics so far evolved rest upon a single premise: that the individual is a member of a community of interdependent parts. The land ethic simply enlarges the boundaries of the community to include soils, waters, plants and animals, or collectively the land.

We need genuine and frequent contact with the natural world to infuse more than self-interest into our short time on the planet. We are wired as such, with a deep connection to Nature, in everyone from generations-proud farmers with hands in the dirt to casual travelers temporarily visiting places grand or humble.

Curt Meine, acclaimed writer and Leopold biographer sporting his own conservationist chops, eloquently explained a common theme in Leopold's commitment to conservation: "Leopold's life story offered insights and lessons that were vital to understanding the roots of conservation and environmental science, policy, and philosophy." On land ethics: "Leopold understood and appreciated recreation as one of the primary ways in which Americans inter-acted with land and the natural world, and through which we could develop a personal land ethic. . . . But he also understood that recreation could also become just one more modern expres-sion of consumption—of taking from the land without regard to its beauty, diversity or health. In other words, the linkage between recreation and conservation was hardly guaranteed."

Meine goes on to discuss Leopold's view on the disconnect of technological advances, our (still developing) relationship with the land, and our place within it. In the grips of an inexorable demand for more access, more convenience, more catered scenery, Leopold saw modern recreation's propensity to separate us from what binds us.

Leopold offers an engaging-yet-simple view of conservation in his writing: "Conservation is the slow and laborious unfolding of a new relationship between people and land." In *A Sand County Almanac*, he shares a conservation esthetic in part with a eulogy to peace and solitude hearkening to the cancerous intrusion of the automobile and its inhabitants into formerly wild places.

> *The automobile has spread this once mild and local predica-ment to the outermost limits of good roads—it has made scarce in the hinterlands something once abundant on the back forty. But that "something" must nevertheless be found. Like ions shot from the sun, the weekenders radiate from every town, generating heat and friction as they go.*

Leopold spent the better part of his life connected to the land, be it in Iowa's Mississippi River Valley, New Mexico's vast forestland, or rural Wisconsin. The breadth of his experience and tireless conservation efforts were complemented by an engaging, honest voice—part rocking chair poet, part scientist—with a rare and beautiful way of connecting through generations. Instead of standing paralyzed in the face of countless environmental travesties, maladies, injustice, and ignorance, Leopold showed us ways to work together in caring for the very place that supports us.

To that end, the Aldo Leopold Foundation was founded in 1982 "with a mission to foster the land ethic through the legacy of Aldo Leopold, awakening an ecological conscience in people throughout the world." Established by Leopold's children, the Baraboo, Wisconsin–based foundation continues their father's inspirational message of an ethical, nurturing, symbiotic relationship between people and Nature. Led with a vision of land stewardship and restoration, the foundation fosters a continuous movement of on-the-ground action complemented with engaging conversation with visitors, landowners, and communities. This intrepid group lives by a mantra of historic preservation, land care, community education, and conservation leadership celebrated annually with Leopold Week—7 days of recognition of Leopold's legacy where people from around the country gather for readings, film viewing, tours, workshops, lectures, and myriad outdoor events including live performances and invasive species removal. It's all-things Aldo and a must-do for your Nature-based bucket list.

Indeed, we would do well to think more like Aldo Leopold. This place in which we live, the only one we have, is "a community to which we belong."

HIS LEGACY

"If the land mechanism as a whole is good then every part is good, whether we understand it or not . . . To keep every cog and wheel is the first precaution of intelligent tinkering."

I can't, nor do I feel the need to, count the hours spent with my dad tinkering in the shop or puttering with some contraption out in the woods, where he always said to keep track of all the parts.

(I sometimes succeeded.) They are indelible memories that shaped who I am; apparently, we had our own Leopold vibe.

Another shared ingredient was the presence of a nearby marsh at our country place, just like Aldo's, filled with some of the same winged beauties. The Marshland Elegy chapter of *A Sand County Almanac* eloquently relates the appearance of cranes at dawn, followed by a simple yet fascinating account of the great birds' place in time.

> *On motionless wing they emerge from the lifting mists, sweep a final arc of sky, and settle in clangorous descending spirals to their feeding grounds. A new day has begun on the crane marsh.*

Leopold goes on to tell us about the peat bog and the cranes "standing upon the sodden pages of their own history." He also reminds us that despite evolutionary millennia, cranes cling to a fragile savior in their fast-disappearing habitat, and the crane is to marsh is to wildness.

> *When we hear his call, we hear no mere bird. We hear the trumpet in the orchestra of evolution. He is the symbol of our untamable past, of that incredible sweep of millennia which underlies and conditions the daily affairs of birds and men.*

His elegy to cranes inspired the Leopold-Pine Island Important Bird Area—16,000 acres of marsh and adjoining ecosystems near Portage, Wisconsin, and home to nearly all of the state's native breeding birds. The Aldo Leopold Foundation carries on its namesake's connection to the land with an array of teaching events, future leaders program, field-based learning, exhibits, hiking trails, and invaluable partnerships with other like-minded organizations. One especially prominent example is the Aldo Leopold Wilderness Research Institute at the University of

Montana–Missoula, a research organization dedicated to wilderness management.

Leopold's legacy also includes the creation of forty-two Wisconsin state trails, from "short-line" routes to big names like the Ice Age Trail, North Country National Scenic Trail, Red Cedar, and Military Ridge. The Leopold Center for Sustainable Agriculture continues working for enduring, low-impact farming practices; and, of course, we are truly fortunate for the opportunity to immerse in his 500 works of writing, from detailed technical reports to prose that tugs heartstrings.

If at no other time you've felt the pull to listen to birdsong from a porch chair or linger in the shade of a big pine, make today that time. Get in touch with the place around you, and your place in it.

BOB MARSHALL

1901–1939

COURTSEY THE WILDERNESS SOCIETY

Anyone who has stood upon a lofty summit and gazed over an inchoate tangle of deep canyons and cragged mountains, of sun-lit lakelets and black expanses of forest, has become aware of a certain giddy sensation that there are no distances, no measures, simply unrelated matter rising and falling without any analogy to the banal geometry of breadth, thickness, and height.

"Gee, this is swell!"

Sentiments of an excitable 1950s kid riding his new bike to the five-and-dime or one of history's most influential conservationists?

Visitors to a particular 1.5-million-acre wilderness area in north-western Montana know the answer. The majority have spoken; nay, they have shouted it from the airy peaks, emerald green valleys, and turquoise alpine lakes littered all over a place known affectionately as the "Bob." Many thousands of discerning outdoor enthusiasts from around the world hold the Bob Marshall Wilderness in great reverence, due in no small part to its namesake and inspiration.

Marshall was a force (a thinker and a doer) with the physical chops and vigor to hike 40 miles on his days off, with a smile every step of the way, complemented by an infectious sense of humor and genuine desire to help others. Born in New York City, Marshall's surroundings—tall buildings, asphalt, and throngs of people—were hardly inspiration for an outdoors lifestyle, but early on he developed an insatiable imagination and verve for the wilderness he read about in books and studied in school. His parents were both proud civil rights activists, and his penchant for the wild world beyond his urban confines was partly educed by his father, a prominent constitutional lawyer and dedicated conservationist.

Marshall was a big fan of Lewis and Clark's expeditions; his parents also helped sow that spirit with yearly family trips to their family cabin in the legendary high country of the Adirondack Mountains, where Marshall would later return with his brother, George, and a friend to climb his first peak. The trio went on to be the first to climb all forty-six of the Adirondacks' highest peaks, a feat that inspired today's Adirondack Forty-Sixers, dedicated to legions of hikers accomplishing the same feat. Through it all, Marshall rarely missed a moment to record all manner of Nature-based statistics and hand-drawn illustrations on his experiences in Nature, a routine that prepared him well for studies at New York State College of Forestry.

Marshall notched nearly perfect grades and a quiver of other *palmarès*, including class secretary, yearbook editor, member of the honor society, track star, and a long record of lake and pond research that earned him the nickname "pond seeker." His academic prowess didn't stop there; he went on to take the civil service test for foresters, turning in the highest score in the nation, and earned a master's in forestry at Harvard. After a stint with the US Forest Service (USFS) researching post-fire forest reproduction in Missoula, Montana, Marshall added to his academic tally with a PhD in plant physiology at Johns Hopkins University.

Marshall was nothing if not versatile—he eventually organized outdoor camps for underprivileged children, studied intricate details of Arctic vegetation, and analyzed fascinating dinner table conversation of lumberjacks with equal zeal. In regard to the latter, in fact, a 1929 edition of *Social Forces* magazine published the results of Marshall's "research study," captivating readers with riveting detail including, "an average of 136 words, unmentionable at church sociables, were enunciated every quarter hour by the hardy hewers of wood."

Moments of zaniness indeed, but Marshall's most visible legacy is the preservation of wilderness. During his Forest Service tenure, he nearly singlehandedly shaped the agency's views and policies on wilderness designation and management. Speaking from the glaring minority, Marshall fervently voted to preserve large tracts of national forest as roadless and undeveloped, echoing a deeply rooted love and concern for Nature that took hold as a young boy.

With generous accolades due for his academic achievements, outdoorsman skills, and tireless passion, it was Marshall's summer vacations that had an especially lasting impact.

Instead of hunkering down to prepare for the homestretch of his doctoral studies, Marshall spent a few months wandering Alaska's wild and unmapped Brooks Range. It was there that he dug in his wilderness preservation heels with concerted efforts to call attention to the region's critical and unspoiled ecological significance, as well as ancillary social research of the roughly one hundred residents scattered about the range. His tireless exploring

GRIZZLY COUNTRY

Montana's Bob Marshall Wilderness Complex is the last vestige grizzly bear habitat in the United States, with roughly 800 of the regal beasts living in the "Bob," as well as Glacier and Yellowstone National Parks. Joining the great bears are endangered gray wolves, elk, deer, bobcats and lynx, mountain goats, bighorn sheep, cougars, and black bear.

would eventually inspire the earliest maps of the area (a significant portion of which would become Gates of the Arctic National Park), names for nearly 200 geographical features still used today, and a pair of popular and informative books. *Arctic Wilderness* (published posthumously in 1956 and as a retitled second edition, *Alaska Wilderness*, in 1970) related tales and vivid description of Alaska's wild country, and *Arctic Village* shared thoughts and findings of his pioneering sociological work with Koyukuk natives. In a rare and grand gesture for the time, Marshall gifted half of *Arctic Village*'s profits to the Koyukuk people.

Alas, Marshall was generally peeved with the absence of accurate and sufficient information on the devastating effects of deforestation, already an epidemic at the start of the 1930s. He channeled his penchant for writing in composing an armload of articles and letters alerting the public to Nature's distress. In fact, his prose came in quite handy throughout his career. To communicate the irreplaceable aesthetic value of wilderness to all of society, Marshall voiced his well-versed and candid thoughts in another book, *The People's Forests*. He leveraged that story's chapters to champion for federal oversight of all of America's forestland in an unwavering effort to find an organization with the chops and inherent mindset to stand up for wilderness preservation—a "permanent American frontier." Lack of initial success did not deter him in the least, and he continued to cultivate powerful and enduring relationships with various governmental organizations and people in strategic, decision-making places.

A great help in Marshall's support of wilderness preservation again came from his own hand in his 1930 *Scientific Monthly* article titled "The Problem of the Wilderness." Prominent natural resources leaders and legions of outdoor enthusiasts celebrated Marshall's unabashed respect and concern for wilderness, stated in language steeped in scientific knowledge as well as from the heart:

> *It is well to reflect that the wilderness furnishes perhaps the best opportunity for pure esthetic enjoyment.*

He genuinely loved being out in the woods or delving into the folds of mountains and fought doggedly to preserve such lands. His determination paid off in grand fashion in 1935, when he infused his own funds to help establish The Wilderness Society. This new group, fortified with Marshall's friendships with the likes of Aldo Leopold, Harvey Broome, and Benton MacKaye, worked diligently to help protect America's wild places—influencing the passage of myriad conservation and public lands bills and purchasing millions of acres of wilderness lands—and is widely regarded as one of the key drivers leading to 1964's signing of the Wilderness Act and formation of the National Wilderness Preservation System. Coinciding with the historical signing was the designation of the Bob Marshall Wilderness Area, in honor of its namesake's dedication to conservation, who believed fully in the importance of Nature to all of us.

"For me, and for thousands with similar inclinations, the most important passion of life is the overpowering desire to escape periodically from the clutches of a mechanistic civilization. To us the enjoyment of solitude, complete independence, and the beauty of undefiled panoramas is absolutely essential to happiness."

As with Leopold, Marshall's adamant views on the place of wilderness was invaluable stimulus for one of America's most galvanizing conservation efforts.

> "There is just one hope of repulsing the tyrannical ambition of civilization to conquer every niche on the whole earth. That hope is the organization of spirited people who will fight for the freedom of wilderness. . . . The preservation of a few samples of undeveloped territory is one of the most clamant issues before us today. Just a few more years of hesitation and the only trace of that wilderness which has exerted such a fundamental influence in molding American character will lie in the musty pages of pioneer books. To avoid this catastrophe demands immediate action."

The Bob Marshall Wilderness Complex includes the Scapegoat and Great Bear Wildernesses and is known as one of the world's most wholly preserved alpine ecosystems. The wilderness system traces both sides of the Continental Divide for 60 miles, highlighted by the enormous Chinese Wall escarpment, 1,000 feet high and dominating 22 miles of the "Bob" and part of the Scapegoat Wilderness. North, south, and middle forks of the Sun and Flathead Rivers wind through the region, packed to the, er, gills with trout that lure fly fishers from around the world. Flanking the rivers are vast tracts of forestland filled with waterfalls, meadows bursting at the seams with a Crayola palette of wildflowers, and hidden alpine lakes.

A priceless treasure indeed, and it does Marshall proud, but the best part is that he didn't stop with this area. He is widely regarded as the inspiration protecting upwards of *5.4 million* acres of America's wild lands. In a new USFS position as chief of the division of recreation and lands, he continued to ramp up his wilderness preservation efforts but did not do so from behind a desk. One of Marshall's trademarks was hiking vast roadless areas during forest inspections in the West and sharing his boots-on-the-ground knowledge with local officials to spark action to preserve lands. Unfortunately the country's already ailing natural resources reflected Marshall's own health, as he battled various illnesses throughout his life. But he never kneeled in surrender to any disease or sickness intent on holding him back. To wit: In 1933, Marshall held simultaneous posts as head of the US government's Division of Forestry and Grazing, and director of the Bureau of Indian Affairs (BIA) Forestry Division. The latter introduced his resolve for cultural equality, especially among Native Americans, whose freedoms and very way of life had been poached before their eyes while the rest of America invaded, for pleasure or (more often) profit, wilderness areas they lived within and nurtured for generations.

Indeed, Marshall wished nothing more than the irreplaceable spirit and beauty of wilderness areas and national parks to be available to all people, and the mid-1930s saw his ingrained ethics become one of the burgeoning wilderness movement's most potent stimuli. He joined the board of the National Parks Association and unleashed salvos of letters and other writings, phone calls, and on-site meetings to all manner of federal agencies, championing for public ownership as the most effective solution toward a sustainable forest industry and wilderness preservation.

For the most part it worked. In the closing chapters of his BIA tenure, Marshall inspired federal management of nearly five million acres of reservation lands as roadless areas, creating sixteen wilderness areas in the process. But it wasn't all rosy; despite his valiant efforts, resorts and recreation areas sprouted, and, with them, all sorts of unpleasant issues Marshall viewed as disparaging to Nature—exploitation of resources, overuse, hordes of people by the car- and trainload, precious natural treasures trampled underfoot, and many resorts banned minorities, which was unacceptable behavior in Marshall's eyes.

Perhaps spurred by such societal changes and constant threat to his wilderness ideals, Marshall returned once again to Alaska in 1938 to continue forest studies related to glaciation's effect on treeline advance, the gradual migration of conifer species to higher elevations. Nine years earlier, he had sown white spruce seeds in a trio of watersheds, but the seeds had not taken hold. Undeterred, he repeated his experiment, along with additional research and adventure forays into Washington and other Alaskan wilderness.

We can only reflect wistfully on what might have been, had Marshall lived a long life with that kind of zeal for wilderness preservation. He died suddenly of heart failure at age 38, far too young for someone bursting with such genuine appreciation for Nature and tireless fight to save it. Nevertheless, he was ahead of his time in fully understanding the tremendous and enduring value of preservation. In homage to his contributions, Marshall's name appears around the country, not only in his namesake wilderness, of course, but in Mount Marshall in the Adirondacks, Marshall Lake in the Brooks Range, college fellowships, and various wilderness conservation initiatives.

HIS LEGACY

We know Bob Marshall as one of the country's earliest and most influential environmentalists, as well as inspiration to later generations of wilderness devotees. He was, of course, much more than that: prophet, collaborator, advocate, fighter, scientist, explorer, and resonating voice for the wild.

> *As society becomes more and more mechanized, it will be more and more difficult for many people to stand the nervous strain, the high pressure, and the drabness of their lives. To escape these abominations, constantly growing numbers will seek the primitive for the finest features of life.*

Abominations of drabness. He was so right in that regard and in how powerful the natural world is in returning the remarkable to our lives. His vision saw miles into the future; he knew the world would fling headlong toward disarray, and fully understood the enduring value of preservation. Perhaps of greatest impact was Marshall's ability to convey that understanding and critical importance to people in his immediate orbit and indeed the American public as a whole.

Several decades after his death in 1939, the USFS adopted Marshall's detailed maps in its establishment of the agency's primitive areas system; his intrepid efforts led directly to establishing The Wilderness Society, which influenced the signing of The Wilderness Act; and in addition to the more than five million acres of protected land attributed to Marshall, he helped establish wilderness camps for underprivileged children. He believed every day in preserving an enriching human experience hosted by Nature, and selflessly toiled to provide it.

The enjoyment of solitude, complete independence, and the beauty of undefiled panoramas is absolutely essential to happiness.

I can state without hesitation it is essential to my happiness, and the feeling pervades among my fellow outdoor-loving brethren trekking way out there in the "Bob" or any other of our country's nearly 800 wilderness areas. And for me, it all starts with a sign.

Planted in the trailside turf, right on the border of wilderness areas across America, are wooden signs of various shapes and sizes. Inscribed upon these signs in bold letters is the name of a wilderness area you are about to enter. In the next few steps, something special happens. The scenery might not immediately look any different, and sounds and smells can be exactly the same, and maybe it's just all in my head; but I feel a great sense of peace in a wilderness, more in step with the personality of the place and at one with its soul.

Not a minute goes by that I don't herald those before me who had the vision and commitment to selflessly work to preserve special places. Marshall's efforts gave us sixty-six wilderness areas made up of more than nine million acres of preserved land, and more designations after his death. Cheers to you, Mr. Marshall. This is swell!

"There is just one hope for repulsing the tyrannical ambition of civilization to conquer every inch on the whole earth. That hope is the organization of spirited people who will fight for the freedom and preservation of the wilderness."

MARGARET MURIE
1902–2003

© NPS ARCHIVES

*Wilderness itself is the basis of all our civilization. I wonder
if we have enough reverence for life to concede to wilderness
the right to live on?*

MARGARET MURIE'S WEDDING DAY WAS ABOUT AS IDYLLIC AS IT
gets. A sunrise ceremony near the Yukon River in the tiny village
of Anvik, Alaska, is not too bad a way to start a life together,
and the new bride had an adventure just getting there. Margaret
joined her mother and maid of honor on an 800-mile trip down-
river from Fairbanks to Anvik, where her beau waited patiently

for her hand. The wedding was romantic and full of promise, but that's where tradition ended. Settle down in a tidy house on a quiet street in town? Hardly. Buzz from their nuptials still heavy in the air, the new couple detached from ordinary with a new spin on honeymoons, packing winter boots and fur parkas for a three-month, 500-mile expedition by dogsled and boat, studying caribou in Alaska's Brooks Range and upper Koyukuk region of the Endicott Mountains. How's that for romance? Not long after that arduous outing, they welcomed their first son and promptly strapped young Martin to a boat and set off on an extended journey down the Old Crow River.

Margaret was born in Seattle but moved with her mother to a small, four-room cabin in rural Fairbanks at age 5, where the mail arrived once a week or so and they had fresh water delivered daily from town in a horse-drawn cart. Margaret promptly took to the area's wild and rugged environs, dogsledding across frozen rivers and lakes at a young age and sowing a pioneer spirit that shaped her as a person and, later, as one of America's most renowned conservationists.

Friends and family took to calling her Mardy, a nickname that accompanied her throughout her vibrant and abundant life. In her late teens, she studied business administration at Simmons College in Boston and returned to finish studies at the Alaska Agricultural College and School of Mines (today's University of Alaska–Fairbanks). Not long after graduating she met Olaus Murie, a Moorhead, Minnesota, native and biologist for the US Bureau of Biological Survey (later becoming the US Fish and Wildlife Service). Olaus was stationed at various remote outposts and, for several years, the young couple relied on letters and occasional meetings to nurture their relationship. Olaus had cultivated a love of the land and its animal inhabitants while exploring the wide open prairie near the Red River, an ethic that served him well in 1927 when the Bureau expanded its study of elk populations in Wyoming's Teton Range and assigned Olaus the task, ushering in a significant change in scenery for the Muries. They moved to Jackson and later to a ranch in Moose, about 15 miles south, raising a trio of children while carrying on field research. Mardy was not a "townie" by any stretch and wanted a place that let her walk out the door and into the woods.

Their honeymoon adventure bond tight as ever, Mardy and Olaus were inseparable. As Olaus collected data and specimens of Wyoming's resident elk, Mardy kept everything in order; in 1945, Olaus accepted the title of director (and, later, president) of The Wilderness Society, a nascent organization dedicated to the protection of existing natural areas and establishment of new wilderness lands. Mardy served as secretary and dove headlong into various conservation efforts protecting America's wilderness areas—she joined Olaus in writing hundreds of newspaper and magazine articles, presenting lectures, and stumping for land protection legislation. The tireless and driven pair also worked on many conservation projects with the Izaak Walton League.

"It is better to be in the thick of the fight than standing in the corner with your face to the wall."

In 1956, Olaus and Mardy embarked on an Alaskan expedition in the Brooks Range that would change their lives and directly influence the future of American wilderness legislation. Intended as an information-gathering venture studying the area's wildlife for potential federal protection, the trip became so much more. Highly regarded zoologist (and, later, a wildlife conservation thought leader) George Schaller joined the Muries on the trip. Just 4 years later, their combined dedication and talents led to the conservation of eight million acres and the establishment of the Arctic National Wildlife Range. The land eventually expanded to more than nineteen million acres and the name changed to Arctic National Wildlife Refuge (ANWR).

The trip and its history-changing result further inspired Mardy, who held strong to and promoted the idea of protecting entire ecosystems, driving the creation of new-look, extra-large parks and reserves around the country. Not surprisingly, however, ANWR's enormous size spawned issues of similar magnitude and complexity, all revolving around money, of course. The loggerheads battle over poking oil drills into ANWR's exquisite and fragile dress has raged for decades, with no end in view.

If Mardy were still with us today, she'd have none of it. With only rare breaks in the action, she partnered with her husband in continuous relation of research findings and their critical importance to congressional decision makers, culminating in the passing of the Wilderness Act of 1964, our environment's brass ring that continues to influence the state of the natural world. Mardy was a proud, front-row attendee at President Lyndon Johnson's signing of the Act, and we can imagine her thinking afterwards of what else could be done in a land conservation light. She was far from finished.

"You are only half a person if you do not care."

Over the next decade, Mardy played a hand in various environmental efforts, including a role with a group sent hither and yon in search of troubled Alaskan lands needing protection from assorted ails. The group's work heralded another resounding win for Nature with the 1980 Alaska National Interest Lands Conservation Act, widely regarded as our country's most significant land preservation venture. The Act consolidated and expanded existing refuges and created new units culminating in nearly eighty million acres of refuge land, with more than twenty-seven million acres as designated wilderness, doubling the size of ANWR in the process.

OPPOSITE: PETE LOMCHID/MOMENT/©GETTY IMAGES

Mardy was a force in a compact package of determined spirit, smiles, and a giving hand, and an exceptional blend of thinker and doer. We can thank her work advocating for conservation in saving our planet's few remaining wilderness areas. She was one of the first women to take the lead in our nation's conservation movement and was deservedly recognized with a trophy case of awards, including the John Muir Award, Robert Marshall Conservation Award, Audubon Medal (a family affair, as it was also presented to Olaus), and the Presidential Medal of Freedom by President Bill Clinton in 1998. Mardy was also bestowed honorary degrees from many universities, and John Denver even wrote and sang a song for her at the Medal of Freedom ceremony.

> "I hope that the United States of America is not so rich that she can afford to let these wildernesses pass by. Or so poor that she cannot afford to keep them."

Mardy Murie, known as the Grandmother of the Conservation Movement, was a powerful voice and lightning rod for Earth's wildest places. To that end, the nonprofit Murie Center was created to ensure continued appreciation for and commitment to Nature, carrying on the Murie family legacy and building on Olaus and Mardy's stalwart foundation. The center, located on the Murie Ranch in Wyoming's Grand Teton National Park, focuses its efforts on paying forward the driving values Mardy held so dear—"respect for Nature, the importance of wilderness, and opportunities for responsible action." The center's assortment of rustic buildings is a designated National Historic Landmark and generously shares the Mardy and Olaus story tying conservation leadership to a genuine land ethic that supports and sustains wild places.

This is the birthplace of the modern conservation movement; today, the Murie Ranch offers an array of programs to "inspire engagement with Nature and connect people to their public lands." Olaus and Mardy viewed this land in the shadow of the Tetons as the heart of American wilderness, and they invited some of conservation's most prominent names to talk over the state of things on their front porch. The Murie Center's Front Porch Conversations carry on the tradition with today's national and local experts in the field gathering to discuss the latest in conservation issues and share inspiration for solutions.

The center also partners with other organizations in offering retreats, training, and related programs, as well as the Teton Sustainability Project promoting an Earth-focused lifestyle in harmony with Nature.

Mardy was a prolific writer. In addition to numerous articles and research reports, she published several books—*Two in the Far North*, *Island Between*, and *Wapiti Wilderness*—and the *Arctic Dance* documentary. One of my favorite parts of *Two in the Far North* is her retelling of the night Fairbanks caught fire. Her father and other townsfolk had to burn the town's bacon supply (not the bacon!) as fuel for the steam-powered water pump. Life as a whole was similarly challenging, with winters clutching the land from October to April and temperatures plummeting for weeks to –50, but Mardy saw it as "an atmosphere of tolerance and love" and verily revered the rugged wilderness around her.

"There may be people who feel no need for nature. They are fortunate, perhaps. But for those of us who feel otherwise, who feel something is missing unless we can hike across land undisturbed only by our footsteps or see creatures roaming freely as they have always done, we are sure there should be wilderness."

HER LEGACY

Margaret Murie lived more than a century and to her last days advocated for the preservation of wild places. Her spirit and

AT WHAT COST?

There might be oil below the surface of the Arctic National Wildlife Refuge to fill billions of barrels. *Might be.* What *is there* is not in question—the unfathomably immense Porcupine caribou herd, North America's largest, with roughly 300,000 members migrating more than 1,500 miles every year between their calving grounds and winter range. It's the longest land migration path of any land mammal on Earth, and the caribou are held sacred by several area Indigenous groups. This regal animal sports enormous antler racks, reaching 4 feet long and wide (growing up to an inch per day!) and weighing in at more than 30 pounds.

legacy shine on no greater stage, perhaps, than the Arctic National Wildlife Refuge—nearly twenty million acres of unspoiled wilderness. Without question, Mardy's name belongs in the same annals as Bob Marshall, Aldo Leopold, Sigurd Olson, and Rachel Carson. She believed that "one of the very few hopes left for man is the preservation of the wilderness" that remains.

She was filled to the brim with curiosity, charisma, and an uncanny ability to bring people together, from all walks of life, to share in celebration of the gift of Nature all around us and propose ways to preserve it. Even after Olaus's passing, Mardy's zeal never waned. After attending the signing of the Wilderness Act, her confidence only grew stronger. She wrote speeches, addressed letters to politicians and key decision makers, and hosted regular visits from family and friends at the Murie Ranch. She especially enjoyed the company of children and young people and held strong faith in younger generations to continue a sound conservation legacy.

Mardy and her in-laws sold the ranch to the National Park Service (today, the property is part of Grand Teton National

Park), but it still buzzes with her spirit. The Teton Science Schools host an annual celebration of conservation leaders honoring people with extraordinary commitment to protecting wilderness and the wildlife within. These leaders receive the Murie Spirit of Conservation Award or Rising Leader Award, recognizing lifetime achievement and dedication to Nature, and exemplary contributions from young people, respectively.

True to form, Mardy passed away at her beloved ranch in Moose, Wyoming, aged 101, her soul still filled with great passion and love for the wild world. In her stead, we have ANWR, one of Earth's most pristine, untrammeled remaining places, with an incredibly rich diversity of ecosystems and hundreds of plant and animal species. Land like this is a rare and beautiful gift, living testament to the persistence and loyalty one person can have, we all can have, in realization of the true wealth in our hands.

DOERS

Sentiment without action is the ruin of the soul.
—*EDWARD ABBEY*

I CAN'T SIT STILL EITHER, ED. NEVER TOOK MUCH TO SITTING around; there's too much to see and places to explore. Like that finely tuned summer day I shimmied into a kayak for an early morning paddle, floating on water so still it felt like the boat was levitating above the surface. I rounded the leeward side of a lily pad plantation and froze, willing my breath and every other body part to stay put, just for a moment. A great blue heron stood near shore, barely visible in a forest of reeds. I stared, it stared back, both of us waiting for the other to flinch. Long moments passed until the bird finally tired of my intrusion and I got my wish; watching avian flight from takeoff is one of my favorite pastimes and this was one for the books. The tall, gangly bird unfolded enormous, delicate, powerful wings and floated upward with a barely audible whisper, painting impromptu silhouettes on the sunrise and my memories.

The scene came to life on a short stretch of reclaimed northern Wisconsin shoreline included in an ambitious lakeshore restoration project. Farsighted residents and state agencies realized the impact of native flora for robust terrestrial and aquatic habitat, and the place bustles with critters today. This is the same kind of

OPPOSITE: MATTEO COLOMBO/DIGITALVISION/©GETTY IMAGES

vision and action inspiring some of our country's most influential environmental crusaders—those who geared up, saddled up, and revved up to go out and literally change the world, in ways disparate in execution but wedded in devotion.

John Muir, for instance, is legendary for indomitable exploits like climbing to the top boughs of a skyscraper pine in a violent storm to experience the elements in all their glory, following 2,000 sheep high into his beloved Sierra Nevada Mountains to commence extended high country rambles, or striding into the maw of an Alaskan glacier wearing a three-piece suit and toting nothing but a blanket, a handful of hardtack, and a canteen, provisions as "unsubstantial as a squirrel's tail." He founded the Sierra Club in 1892 and was instrumental in the National Park Service's establishment 24 years later. Muir's name is synonymous with conservation, and he is widely regarded as America's most famous environmental champion.

Sharing similar accolades is Rachel Carson, an unassuming marine biologist with the chops to challenge the deeply seated (dimwitted) perception of human mastery over Nature. She virtually singlehandedly eradicated the use of DDT and other beastly pesticides through her message in *Silent Spring*, saving the bald eagle from impending extinction and igniting a global environmental movement that inspired the Environmental Protection Agency and Environmental Defense Fund.

Sigurd Olson grew up in northern Wisconsin's woods and later became a wilderness guide in the mystical Quetico-Superior border country of Minnesota and Ontario. He penned ten books and fought passionately for the environment for decades. Around the same time, Edward Abbey was out mingling with cactus and cliffrose in the Desert Southwest or tantalizing us with writing equal parts anarchy and lyrical, all in staunch defense for the wilderness. Up north, way up north, Will Steger traveled unfathomable miles by dogsled, snowshoes, and skis to show us the fragile, unsung, glorious, interminable beauty of the land of ice and cold.

His kinship with and respect for Nature continues unabated after five decades of climate change study and a host of polar exploration firsts.

What does this all mean to us? For anyone who loves a desert sunrise or high mountain peak, the salty allure of the sea or an eagle in resplendent flight, the people in these chapters had a lot to do with it. They wrote, studied, traveled, and afforded strong voice in support and celebration of the places that mean the most, that mean everything. Here's to the doers and the path they forged—let's follow their lead.

JOHN MUIR

1838–1914

H20557 U.S. COPYRIGHT OFFICE

Keep close to Nature's heart . . . and break clear away, once in a while, and climb a mountain or spend a week in the woods. Wash your spirit clean.

EIGHT HUNDRED MILES BY CANOE FROM ALASKA'S WRANGELL Island to Glacier Bay and back, punctuating the return trip traversing treacherous miles on foot across glaciers. Throw in an ink-black night lost among bottomless-pit crevasses for good measure. Climbing to the highest boughs of a 100-foot Douglas fir to better experience the fury of a winter storm. "Nature was holding high festival and every fiber of the most rigid giants thrilled with glad excitement."

Riding an avalanche from the rim of Yosemite Valley. Climbing onto a 3-inch-wide rock crag at the crest of Yosemite Falls to get a better view. Setting off on a thousand-mile walk from Indiana to the Gulf of Mexico en route to explore the Amazon. "My plan was simply to push on in a general southward direction by the wildest, leafiest and least trodden way I could find, promising the greatest extent of virgin forest," John Muir wrote in *A Thousand-Mile Walk to the Gulf.*

Any one of these could be life-list adventures for the rest of us, but Muir sought them out as everyday outings, and they became his lifeblood from a young age. Even his name is entrenched in wilderness; Muir in Scottish means a moor or wild land, perfectly suited for a bloke with such a fondness for all things outdoors. Born in Dunbar, Scotland, Muir lived with his family near the North Sea, conveniently bursting with shore birds, crabs skittering among rocks on the shore, eels, critter-filled seaweed and—best of all—the ragged ruins of Dunbar Castle. He got to know Nature by digging in the sand, watching and listening to sea life, and accompanying his grandfather on regular walks near the water or ambling through hayfields. In sight or sound, smell or touch, wilderness was everywhere and if not in the immediate vicinity, Muir counted the hours until Saturday arrived when he could run off to the sea or an empty field or even spy on what was happening in an unkempt town garden. Anywhere to revel in "the fullness of Nature's glad wildness."

At age 11 in 1849, Muir's family picked up stakes and emigrated to America, a harrowing, 6-week trip by sea to the docks of New York harbor. But the trip was far from over when the ship dropped anchor; they shuffled their belongings to another vessel and traveled across the Great Lakes to Milwaukee, Wisconsin, where they eventually settled on an 80-acre farmstead near Portage, which they dubbed Fountain Lake Farm. The country at the time was very much a frontier environment, and Muir saw their home in the same light, quickly taking to exploring every inch of the place and spreading his wings in surrounding forests. From *The Story of My Boyhood and Youth*: "Oh, that glorious Wisconsin wilderness! Everything new and pure in the very prime of the spring when Nature's pulses were beating highest and mysteriously keeping time with our own!"

Alas, the world wasn't all sunshine and light. Muir watched environmental degradation in real time as crop harvest yields shrunk from years of shortsighted and harebrained farming practices. Muir's father recognized the malady as well, seeing many of their fellow farmers denude lands to breaking points. Eight years after settling at Fountain Lake, the Muir family picked up stakes, moved to a new parcel 5 miles east, and started all over again. Toiling anew, the young John continued feeding a voracious appetite for learning, waking in the middle of the night to read books of all kinds.

He later took that verve to the University of Wisconsin where he studied chemistry and botany, and discovered the philosophy of Ralph Waldo Emerson, an influence that would help shape his wanderlust and his mind. Indeed, illuminating botany lessons and a hardscrabble youth exploring Wisconsin's countryside instilled a ravenous attraction to exploring, but Muir never felt satiated. What better way to fill the void than a long walk? At the time, Muir worked as a sawyer in Indianapolis and, after a period of personal unrest, he decided he needed to see the rainforest. He gathered his savings, threw a few provisions into a sack, and began walking, intent on reaching South America to discover his calling or other manifest of life meaning. For 1,000 miles, he collected plants and surveyed his surroundings all the way to Florida until malaria upended the trip. He rested a bit before continuing on to Cuba, but the illness proved too much, forcing a change in plans in the form of another boat ride to New York.

Muir didn't stay in the Big Apple long; instead, he followed the pull of a fateful move west in the late 1860s. He boarded a schooner from New York to Panama and then on to the California coast, followed by walking to the foothills of the Sierra Nevada. It was here that Muir established his conservation roots and "unconditionally surrendered" to Nature. He respected and adored wilderness, not simply for the fun of it, but delving deep into woods or the innards of a glacier or scaling high mountains to become truly acquainted with their ancestry and inner workings. He then shared those wanderings in stimulating prose, such as the effect crafted after seeing a then-active glacier at Alaska's Stickeen Fiord: "No words can convey anything like an adequate conception of its sublime grandeur. Still more impotent are words in telling the peculiar awe one experiences in entering these mansions of the icy north." From his journals:

I only went out for a walk and finally concluded to stay out till sundown, for going out, I found, was really going in.

And Muir went in, nearly every day of his life, afraid of nothing and wholly at peace in the wilderness. The Sierra offered endless miles of canyons, rivers, high peaks, and valleys, and he plunged headlong into it all, often stretching his physical limits to just this side of calamity, intentionally surrounding himself for months at a time with Nature's vigor and spiritual light. Muir worked as a sheepherder for a summer before landing a job building a sawmill in the Yosemite Valley, quickly establishing a home there and then regularly leaving it to roam on self-imposed quests to explore every mountain summit, canyon, nook, and cranny in the valley. He soon became known as John o' the Mountains, but glaciers were perhaps Muir's greatest delight; he was attracted to them like a little kid to a sledding hill. His exhaustive studies and explorations cemented his place as a critical pioneer in America's nascent understanding of glaciers' icy realms. In fact, the general public had no idea glaciers lived in the folds of Yosemite's mountains until Muir discovered them and convinced the masses that

YOSEMITE'S TWIN

Millions of visitors descend upon Yosemite National Park every year, but relatively few are aware a twin of the park's legendary valley, born of the same glacial artistry some 10,000 to 15,000 years ago, lies just 15 miles north—albeit in a much-altered state. Home to Native Americans for many thousands of years before white settlers appeared on the scene, Hetch Hetchy Valley was one of Earth's most extravagantly beautiful places, with protection "in perpetuity" as part of the national park. But not so fast; in arguably the biggest environmental blunder in US history, President Woodrow Wilson signed a bill allowing San Francisco to pillage the valley for its own use. Nationwide controversy erupted but the city got its way; a big, ugly dam was built, flooding the valley and desecrating a place of exquisite beauty and rich history. A bitter defeat for Muir and millions of Americans, the melee ignited a global conservation movement and efforts are underway today to restore Hetch Hetchy. The American people deserve it.

rivers of ice carved Yosemite Valley and other spectacular natural treasures around the world.

Through it all, Muir had a special fondness for Alaska, a place he considered the definitive wilderness and living laboratory for many of his discoveries of glaciers and their behaviors. Muir was fascinated (and who wouldn't be?) with examining glaciers *while they moved*. He once paddled a kayak among enormous, raggedy icebergs and was so enthralled he failed to notice they were closing together. He escaped with little room to spare but the experience only further stimulated his attraction to the wilds.

He reveled in adventure and discovery, immersing himself in learning all there was to know about a delicate flower or the unfathomable, scouring weight of a glacier. From the woods or his desk at home, Muir wrote prolifically on preserving natural landscapes, rapidly gaining public popularity while simultaneously calling attention to rampant destruction of woodlands, waterways, and fragile mountain ecosystems throughout the West and Alaska. Muir then capped off his studies by traveling constantly and lobbying governments with equal zeal, eventually capturing time with Teddy Roosevelt, treating the president to a tour of the Yosemite region to show firsthand the effects of resource exploitation and Nature's critical cog in the grand scheme. Again from Muir's journals:

When we try to pick out anything by itself, we find it hitched to everything else in the Universe.

Roosevelt accompanied Muir on a three-night camping trip, widely regarded as the most significant in conservation history, where perhaps around a campfire or atop a high overlook, Muir persuaded the president to include Yosemite as a national park. (The park was formally established in 1906.) The backcountry foray made an impression on Roosevelt, set aside one of America's most revered parks, and fueled Muir's preservation drive to protect other places such as the Petrified Forest, Grand Canyon, and allocate land for Sequoia, Mount Rainier, and General Grant National Parks.

Not a bad wilderness trophy case but there was still much to explore and work required to shield the places he loved from compromise. Muir has been anointed with titles such as wizened prophet, shepherd, and Father of the National Parks, but at heart he was a doer. Unfortunately, he consistently battled a pervasive mindset that man was above Nature, with the "right" to do with it as he pleased. Ironically, this mirrored the sermons of Muir's Calvinist father about man's dominion over all else. Muir thought otherwise, that our place is equal to Nature, not above, and a militant note crept into his writing,

Why should man value himself as more than a small part of the one great unit of creation?

The wrongs done to trees, wrongs of every sort, are done in the darkness of ignorance and unbelief, for when the light comes, the heart of the people is always right.

He called out this atrocious and ultimately destructive arrogance in his journals, exclaiming that "men are painfully astonished whenever they find anything which they cannot eat or render in some way they call useful to themselves." Muir seemed surlier as the passage continued, writing that even "noxious and insignificant" creatures originate from God and are thus our fellows. "The fearfully good of modern civilization cry 'heresy' on everyone whose sympathies reach a single hair's breadth beyond the boundary epidermis of our own species."

That's telling it like it is, but Muir's strongest attribute was showing Nature to the world through tangible facts and explanations of what he studied and learned in the wild. In fact, he was so adept at the practice that the Smithsonian Institution requested his reports from extended research outings, and even sternly traditional geologists eventually came around. Muir continued fighting for responsible forest management in Yosemite and other regions, noting the sickening destruction of logging in pronouncements like this: "The practical importance of the preservation of our forests is augmented by their relations to climate, soil and streams." Sounds like a message appropriate for today as well, doesn't it?

Muir's determined actions and eloquent words managed great things, however, among salvos of adversity. The Sierra Club, inspired largely from Muir's work, elected him as president (a post he held until his death); he advised future US Forest Service officials on protecting millions of acres of protected lands and ushered in a worldwide conservation movement. He filled his journals with accounts of scintillating northern lights, observations on the celestial world, and nuances of resident wildlife habitat. His eyes caught the little things, too, like the previously unknown *Erigeron* plant from the Cape Thompson region, subsequently named in his honor.

But things turned volatile back home in California. In the early 1900s, Muir faced a formidable foe. San Francisco needed water, and officials looked to Yosemite's Hetch Hetchy Valley to get it. In America's first grassroots lobbying effort, Muir led a valiant fight to save the valley, his most beloved retreat and every bit as beautiful and precious as Yosemite proper, from being swallowed by the backwash of a colossal cement doorstop.

Dam Hetch Hetchy! As well dam for water-tanks the people's cathedrals and churches, for no holier temple has ever been consecrated by the heart of man.

The ensuing battle between preservation and conservation camps consumed more than a decade, ending in defeat for the valley. Muir died one year after completion of the O'Shaughnessy Dam, but its construction lit a spark of national recognition of the importance and place of Nature and its resources. Bickering among disparate interest groups continues today. The Sierra Club, Restore Hetch Hetchy, and many others favor proposals to decommission the dam and restore the valley toward its original state. The process would take many decades, of course, but the argument is sound that the valley belongs to the American people, not private entities. Competing views claim the dam remains a source of hydroelectric power and removal of the structure would be an economic train wreck. Time will tell.

For all his accomplishments and influence, John Muir was not without blemish. Some accounts paint Muir in a racist light or make mention of disparaging comments toward Indigenous and other peoples, supported by recent articles and announcements from the Sierra Club, *New York Times*, and other national publications. An opinion that Muir carried a distorted view of conservation also pervades some camps, calling out his proclamations of Yosemite as wild and pristine and "no mark of man is visible upon it." Man had, of course, already made his mark there; however, treading lightly, visible evidence was not in plain sight. Native Americans knew this place as the Ahwahnee Valley, and they and their successors called it home for thousands of years. Its Eden-like appearance is a result of their purposeful stewardship of the forest; they respected the valley for its resources and wholly relied on them. Indeed, the very idea of conservation was acknowledged and practiced long before it became a "movement."

These are intriguing and worthwhile conversations, indeed; but for the scope of this book, many of our country's most revered natural places exist from Muir's considerable contribution and he is celebrated in this book as such. There is no debating the presence and drive of generations of conservationists carrying on Muir's efforts. His influence is still of great import today and his voice remains resonant in defense of our lingering wild places.

Occasionally maligned for being impractical or elitist in his single-minded focus to preserve "little pieces of wilderness," Muir was nothing if not inspirational and passed on a lesson to step back and take heed of our relationship with Nature.

"I am hopelessly and forever a mountaineer."

HIS LEGACY

John Muir's impact is without question. He was the lightning rod of the modern conservation movement and, arguably, endures as America's most influential and famous naturalist. His efforts more than 150 years ago still resonate today; his words inspire with as much lyrical sway as the day they were written. He was a fiercely devoted adventurer, renowned writer, and tireless defender of wilderness.

Through his writing and detailed scientific study, Muir persuaded the US government to establish Yosemite, Sequoia, Mount Rainier, and Grand Canyon as national parks, along with a collection of national monuments. He was a consummate explorer with a tin cup, dry bread, and a will to defend the places he loved, with an unwavering belief that Nature is at once delicate, vulnerable, spectacular, selfless, and generous.

"Thousands of tired, nerve-shaken, over-civilized people are beginning to find out that going to the mountains is going home; that wildness is a necessity." (*Our National Parks*)

"The battle for conservation will go on endlessly. It is part of the universal warfare between right and wrong." (*The Yosemite*)

We can thank John Muir for our national parks and many millions of acres in national forests across the country, and his name appears in places from coast to coast—Muir Woods, Muir Trail, Muir Glacier, and dozens more. His home in Martinez, California, is a national historical monument, attracting nearly 30,000 visitors every year. Alaska alone is filled with homages to Muir, including Glacier Bay National Park, Admiralty Island National Monument, Muir Glacier, Misty Fjords National Monument, and other wilderness areas in Tongass National Forest.

But his greatest legacy is out there, the places he helped preserve, places where we can follow his footsteps into wilderness grace.

GEORGE WASHINGTON CARVER

1864–1943

PHOTOGRAPHS BY FRANCES BENJAMIN JOHNSTON

Ninety-nine percent of the failures come from people who have the habit of making excuses.

GEORGE WASHINGTON CARVER WAS THE ORIGINAL MR. PEANUT. If you're not familiar with his name, you are with his products. Over the course of a nearly 50-year career, Carver developed a laundry list of peanut-based goods many of us use every day, like milk, Worcestershire sauce, shaving cream, skin lotion, wood stain, antiseptic, laxatives, paper, insulation, dyes, soap, linoleum, cosmetics, and plastics. And don't forget kitchen standbys flour and vinegar, derived from sweet potatoes, along with other handy items like molasses, ink, and postage stamp glue. Popular belief in some circles has Carver as the inventor of peanut butter as well, but that accomplishment goes to the Incas from around 950 BC, who regularly ground peanuts into a paste, most likely for eating and likely other ingenious uses.

Here in the United States, Carver led the peanut-y way, eventually developing more than 300 products in the food, industrial, and commercial realms, and was widely known as "The Peanut Man." This all developed from an insatiable hunger to learn the intrinsic abilities of plant life, and his knack for agriculture also led to the discovery and implementation of crop rotation, one of the country's earliest iterations of ag-based resource awareness.

Carver's story is equal parts astonishing, brave, and despicable. He was born on a farm in the vicinity of Diamond, Missouri, 1 year prior to the abolishment of slavery. His heritage, however, reached back a decade or so into the country's tumultuous slavery era. Moses Carver, a white man and owner of a 240-acre farm, is said to have been against slavery but needed hands to work the property. One of his strategies included the purchase of a 13-year-old girl named Mary, who would later give birth to George at a young age. We don't know much about George's father other than he was likely a field hand killed in a farming accident long before George's birth.

Stories from the time tell us that life on the Carver farm, while deplorable from a slavery perspective, was generally adequate for Mary until the earliest, innocent months of George's life. A band of Confederate slave raiders oozed around Missouri at the time, pilfering defenseless families with young children from random farmsteads and selling or trading them in other locations. One day, the raiders descended on the Carver farm and kidnapped George and his mother and sister, hauling them off to

Kentucky, where they were sold like everyday objects. Outraged and determined to retrieve young George and his family, Moses sent a neighbor to find them and deliver a raider reckoning. The trusty neighbor eventually tracked down only George and finagled a trade of one of Moses's prized horses for the boy.

Thrilled to have George back on the farm, Moses and his wife, Susan, intended to return the young child to everyday labor, but George was a frail lad, plagued with nearly constant sickness, and too weak to carry out physically demanding chores. Susan took a liking to and saw promise in George and eschewed outdoor farm work in favor of teaching him more manageable tasks such as laundry, cooking, embroidery, gardening, and drumming up homemade herbal remedies.

Susan's kitchen lessons proved fortuitous in the life of The Peanut Man, as George dove headlong into learning all he could about plants, their benefits, and yet unknown product applications. The home kitchen became a part-time laboratory for experimenting with soil conditioners, pesticides, and various fungus-fighting chemicals used by area farmers. Still under 10 years old, Carver displayed a keen grasp of techniques identifying the health and potential yield of a crop field, orchard, or even small household garden, and his reputation as the "plant doctor" quickly spread throughout the region.

Moses and Susan recognized his talents and found an all-black school in Neosho, southeast of Joplin, that accepted George into their programs. He walked 10 miles to the school several days a week, but quickly became unfulfilled and frustrated with the quality of education and left the farm to seek a better life. He spent the next 10 years moving between towns all over the Midwest, eventually settling in Minneapolis, Kansas, and working in domestic roles to earn money for tuition at the local high school. After graduation, Carver worked as a ranch hand for a while and then with the railroad, saving every penny for college. The hard work paid off in 1888 when Simpson College in Iowa accepted him as its first-ever African-American student. Initially studying toward a teaching degree, Carver was urged by one of his instructors to consider a botany degree at Iowa State Agricultural School (today's Iowa State University). Carver accepted the challenge and his passion for learning was an ideal fit:

> *Education is the key to unlock the golden door of freedom.*
> *Learn to do common things uncommonly well; we must always keep in mind that anything that helps fill the dinner pail is valuable.*

Carver had found his way, excelling at things like fungal infections in soybean plants. In 1894, he became the school's first African American to earn a Bachelor of Science degree. Better yet, department professors were so impressed with his work they asked him to continue graduate studies as part of the faculty, and he soon became director of the Iowa State Experimental Station, working alongside other noted scientists studying plant diseases.

In the midst of research and agriculture application, Carver discovered two new fungus species, dabbled in nitrogen depletion studies, and established notoriety as a leading industry scientist en route to earning a master's degree in agriculture. He had hardly hung his diploma on the wall when offers poured in, one of which arrived from Alabama's Tuskegee Institute to run its new agricultural school. Carver would receive two living quarters rooms (one to live in and one for plant specimens) and the title of department director. Carver accepted and spent his entire career at the school.

"There is no short cut to achievement. Life requires thorough preparation—veneer isn't worth anything."

Not everything was rosy, however. Agriculture study was hardly mainstream, and the school expected a great deal from

Carver, including teaching, keeping restrooms functioning, sitting on various boards and committees, and managing the school's farms. This didn't leave much time to devote to his true passion—researching different agricultural practices that would help poor farmers of the South. This is where Carver's laboratory prowess proved most valuable. He discovered that decades of growing cotton in the same fields siphoned away valuable nutrients, inspired rampant erosion, and left farmers with low yields. But Carver realized that nitrogen-fixing plants (sweet potatoes, peanuts, soybeans) could restore soil health and help replanted cotton grow like gangbusters. He also showed farmers the monetary and environmental benefits of feeding hogs acorns in place of commercial choices and replacing fertilizer with swamp sludge to augment soil.

Area farmers were ecstatic and celebrated Carver's name with every new planting season. Carver furthered the cause by developing the Jesup Wagon, a mobile, horse-drawn classroom that brought crop rotation lessons directly to sharecroppers. The innovative program, named after a noted Tuskegee donor, was a huge success, reaching more than 2,000 people every month in its first season. Instead of spending their meager funds buying fertilizer and other everyday necessities, Carver encouraged farmers to look to the land. He provided poor Black farmers a reason and the tools they needed to stay on their land.

But with crop rotation in full swing and cotton yields rebounding, farmers had enormous stocks of peanuts sitting around. This was Carver's call to hole up in his lab and develop all those ancillary uses for peanuts, which he introduced to the public through everyday advertising brochures, essentially saving the South's agriculture economy in the process. Indeed, his influence and on-the-ground advances turned peanuts into a $200 million per year crop industry and Alabama's leading export.

Thus began a succession of big moments in Carver's career and our country's history. In the heat of World War I, rubber

THE MOVEABLE SCHOOL

With Tuskegee Institute founder Booker T. Washington's call to faculty to "take their teaching into the community," George Washington Carver designed a student-built movable school, the Jesup Wagon. First transported by horses, succeeding wagon iterations became motorized trucks. Later, the Booker T. Washington Agricultural School on Wheels brought a group of educators to rural areas, teaching self-sufficiency through innovative agriculture.

was in short supply and the US government asked him to help Henry Ford develop an alternative. The war also made it difficult to secure dyes, but Carver was there to assist domestic textile corporations by creating "homegrown" dyes made from Alabama soil. He touted the benefits of massages with peanut oil as a potential polio vaccine (the prescription provided only temporary relief of paralysis) and, among many widely used commercial products, who can forget his peanut nitroglycerine concoction? He was on to something, indeed, as peanut oil can make glycerol, a key ingredient in nitroglycerine, which in turn is used in dynamite.

Carver's contributions cemented his legacy as one of our country's most prominent scientists, and his work didn't go unnoticed. He was named as Speaker for the US Commission on Interracial Cooperation, for example, as well as the USDA's head of the Division of Plant Mycology and Disease Survey. Carver presented a speech on behalf of the newly established Peanut Growers Association of America, urging Congress to pass a tariff law protecting the industry from an influx of imported crops. Teddy Roosevelt called on him for nationwide agriculture advice. President Franklin D. Roosevelt signed an order creating a monument to Carver (located in Diamond, Missouri). He was posthumously inducted into the National Inventors Hall of Fame.

The US Post Office issued commemorative postage stamps, and a pair of our country's military ships are named for him. An array of schools and scholarships also carry his name, and January 5 is now George Washington Carver Recognition Day.

His recognition carried beyond America's boundaries, as well. In 1916, the British Royal Society of Arts named Carver a member. He also assisted Mahatma Gandhi with nutrition matters and agriculture education, and many foreign governments sought his advice, including an invitation from Joseph Stalin to oversee Russian cotton plantations. (Carver refused.)

With little guidance or support from a very young age, Carver put his shoulder to the wheel and initiated ideas and approaches on sustainability far ahead of their time. Selfless to the end, upon his death he donated his life savings to establishing Tuskegee University's Carver Research Foundation in continuation of sustainable agricultural research.

HIS LEGACY

"Nothing is more beautiful than the loveliness of the woods before sunrise."

On rare occasions, we are blessed with someone who dedicates the whole of his life to helping others and the physical world supporting all of us. George Washington Carver covered both bases, indifferent to his generation's racial unrest, instead intent on serving the needs of downtrodden humanity, establishing hope for a livable future and establishing agriculture sustainability practices that changed the face of the industry. His pioneering crop rotation theories remain rooted on farms around the world, contributing not only to high produce yields but also alleviating damaging erosion events and "dead" soil with little strength to support life.

His work ushered in historic advances in agriculture training and practice and an entirely new outlook on responsible resource use while boosting crop diversity, fine-tuning farm practices, and bringing soil conservation to light. Through it all, Carver became a stalwart symbol of influential achievements by African Americans, instilling pride and hope, encouragement to follow dreams, and even the support and respect of a largely prejudiced white America. In addition to honors including the George Washington Carver Museum (part of the National Park Service), and George Washington Carver National Monument, Carver's childhood home was the first named in honor of an African American.

"When you do the common things in life in an uncommon way, you will command the attention of the world."

SIGURD OLSON

1899–1982

COURTSEY THE MINNESOTA HISTORICAL SOCIETY

*No greater challenge faces us than to preserve some places of
quiet and beauty for the sanity of mankind.*

THE QUETICO-SUPERIOR WILDERNESS INCLUDES MORE THAN
five million acres of primeval lands doused with thousands of
lakes, glacier-carved river gorges, bogs, and boreal forest pulsing
with life. Words in traditional form are tragically deficient to
describe the spirit of this place, its beauty, ecological significance,
and rich history. The land sprawls across the US-Canada border
between northeastern Minnesota and Ontario, perpetually linking

them in Nature's gracious embrace of Voyageurs National Park, the Boundary Waters Canoe Area Wilderness, Superior National Forest, Lake Superior Highlands, and Quetico Provincial Park.

Immersed in it all was Sigurd Olson, the most celebrated among Minnesota's pantheon of Nature writers. At a glance in his elder years, he looked the quintessential northern woodsman— warm, half smile on his weathered face, wavy gray hair under a faded fedora, and flannel coat blending with the trees. Smoke from a well-worn pipe swirls around the scene; throw in an air of poetry and you'd hardly guess Olson was one of our country's conservation giants.

Born in Chicago in 1899, the Olson family moved north to Sister Bay near the tip of Wisconsin's Door Peninsula, where Sigurd nurtured a love of exploring pine forests and along the sandy shoreline. The family later moved to Ashland, and after high school Olson enrolled at Northland College, a respected environment-focused school. During two invigorating college years, he spent much of his free time fishing, boating, hunting, and otherwise feeding an outdoors spirit before traveling south to finish undergraduate studies at the University of Wisconsin–Madison. He followed up with a master's in animal ecology at the University of Illinois, focusing his work on the timber wolf, a venerable symbol of the North Country and portent of things to come.

Following grad school, Olson moved closer to the wolves, taking a high school teaching position in Ely, Minnesota, a rough-and-tumble mining town in the state's Iron Range. (Ely today is also home to the world-renowned International Wolf Center.) Olson taught biology at the high school for several years and then transferred to the faculty at Ely Junior College (now Vermillion Community College) as a professor and later dean of the school, a post he held for a decade. During these nascent years up north, Olson worked as a canoe guide and soon evolved into a respected and accomplished outfitter, escorting visitors into the boundary waters area for 30 years.

This was also the place where he began to write about the wild, watery world around him. His first published article in a 1921 edition of the *Milwaukee Journal* related a northern canoe expedition. Olson went on to write nine acclaimed books on the outdoors, from woods to water to the divine. He was enamored, as well, with mystical happenings overhead. If you've never seen the northern lights, for example, consider this eloquent description from *The Singing Wilderness*, arguably his most popular tome:

> *The lights of the aurora moved and shifted over the horizon. Sometimes there were shafts of yellow tinged with green, then masses of evanescence which moved from east to west and back again. Great streamers of bluish white zigzagged like a tremendous trembling curtain from one end of the sky to the other. Streaks of yellow and orange and red shimmered along the flowing borders. Never for a moment were they still, fading until they were almost completely gone, only to dance forth again in renewed splendor with infinite combinations and startling patterns of design.*

Along with lyrical charisma like that, Ely also inspired Olson's career as an active, avid conservationist, the roots of which date back to the 1920s. He believed that spiritual encounters in and with wilderness were vital to the success of modern society and worked valiantly to ensure both sides of that relationship received equal attention. In 1947, he resigned from teaching to dedicate himself wholly to conservation and writing, complementing disciplines where his endeavors are as enviable in scope as they are in substance.

By now, Olson was entrenched in the exceptional beauty and mystique of the far north, largely still intact thanks to decades of farsighted vision before him. Records show the efforts of Minnesota Forestry Commissioner Christopher Andrews helped remove more than 640,000 acres of land from public sale in the early

1900s, and Andrews continued similar lobbying, after a border route canoe trip at age 77, to establish an international forest reserve that would become the Quetico-Superior.

With all things environment, of course, come debate, political scrapping, and vehement exchanges of opinion in the struggle to strike a balance between wilderness preservation, commercial interests, and recreation. Around 1920, the US Forest Service's Arthur Carhart submitted a recreation plan for the Superior National Forest, essentially Olson's back yard, favoring primitive use. A new proposal soon followed, presented by tourism and logging industries determined to build roads into the region. Fortunately, a compromise of sorts resulted in the Superior Roadless Area. But pressures didn't abate.

Olson took to the fight to keep the Quetico-Superior free of roads and dams; in fact, his work helped secure an order by Secretary of Agriculture William Jardine restricting road construction in sensitive areas. Olson was also instrumental in preservation efforts, such as the Shipstead-Newton-Nolan Act of 1930, limiting logging activities and altogether forbidding private enterprise to alter natural water levels.

"By saving any wilderness, what you are really saving is the human spirit."

Olson went on to serve as a wilderness ecologist for the Izaak Walton League, president of the National Parks Association for eight years, vice president and president of The Wilderness Society for another eight years, and National Park Service advisor for more than 10 years. In one of conservation's most visible and seminal moments, Olson orchestrated a fight in the 1940s to ban air flight into Minnesota's border country, sparking a national throwdown among activists, private landowners, and commercial industries.

WATER WAYS

Bring your sea legs. Voyageurs National Park is a 200,000-acre wilderness gem in far northern Minnesota, hugging the Canadian border. The park's best attribute is it's not easy to get to. More than a third of the park is accessible only by water (in warm months), be it the trio of big lakes on three sides—Rainy, Kabetogama, and Namakan—or tentacles of tributary creeks, rivers, and smaller lakes. Established in 1975, the park boasts some of the wildest and geologically rich ecosystems in the country, filled with mystical boreal forest, loon calls, northern lights, and wolf tracks. In the late 1600s, demand for beaver pelts sparked a lively fur trade attracting rugged voyageurs (fur traders) who later inspired the park's name.

Olson's don't-back-down approach persuaded President Truman to grant reserved air space over the area, subsequently inspiring the Boundary Waters Canoe Area Wilderness in 1978.

Olson continued publishing engaging stories in a collection of books including *Listening Point*, *Reflections from the North Country*, *Songs of the North*, and *Wilderness Days*, endearing a loyal following that is wider than ever today. Taking breaks between chapters, he helped compose the Wilderness Act of 1964, preserving millions of acres of wild lands in the process, and offered his voice in establishing the Arctic National Wildlife Refuge and other remote and vibrant Alaskan lands that became part of the Alaska National Interest Lands Conservation Act. He was there in the formation of Voyageurs National Park and California's Point Reyes National Seashore. His lifelong work earned highest honors from the country's most prominent conservation organizations including The Wilderness Society, Sierra Club, and National Wildlife Foundation. Olson had an impact abroad, as well, teaching in the zoology department at England's American Army University.

When it comes to summarizing Olson, former Sierra Club presidents Edgar Wayburn and George Marshall perhaps said it best. Wayburn: "He was the personification of the wilderness defender. He was trusting and sentimental, but also a strong leader who could bring together warring factions of environmentalists." Marshall: "He made wilderness and life sing."

Olson's biographer David Backes adds, "Olson was, in many respects, a second John Muir. The similarities are striking. Muir's theology, like Olson's, arose out of direct, joy- and wonder-filled experiences in Nature, with subsequent reflection and reading giving form and adding nuances to those experiences. And Muir's evangelism, like Olson's, was devoted to helping people discover the sacredness of creation and their own connectedness to it."

High praise indeed but sentiments not shared with all. Many people in Olson's own hometown outright blamed wilderness regulations for hog-tying the local economy. In an especially unsettling display of poor taste, opponents hung effigies of Sierra Club members, including Olson, at a hearing on granting wilderness designation to the Boundary Waters Canoe Area. Many in these raucous groups were pro-logging or in favor of motorized vehicle access, complaining that the hundreds of thousands of acres already accessible at the time weren't enough. Naturally, Olson felt trapped in a sense, in the face of so much hostility and threats upon the wilderness places that shaped his life. Nevertheless, he continued sharing a philosophy and, like Aldo Leopold, a land ethic that deeply touched those around him.

"Joys come from simple and natural things: mists over meadows, sunlight on leaves, the path of the moon over water."

He was staunch in his belief that humanity's basic needs are rooted in the ancient environment shaping the evolution of our species. This focus on values became his trademark, and it rang true in his writing.

If we can change our priorities, achieve balance and understanding in our roles as human beings in a complex world, the coming era can well be that of a richer civilization, not its end.

He certainly had no shortage of inspiration, steeped in centuries-old history and tradition. The Rainy Lake and Pigeon River watersheds were part exploration canvas, part lifeline for generations of American Indians and the intrepid voyageurs who followed. Following time-tested methods in place from Ojibwe culture, voyageurs, French for "traveler," were tough-as-nails French-Canadian traders moving furs and other goods from suppliers to inland peoples, often paddling at speed for upwards of 15 hours a day and portaging ridiculously long distances. The Montreal to Grand Portage trip was a common route, requiring six weeks, and then continuing upstream along the riverways.

Olson surely had a voyageur streak, and what he lacked in brawn he made up for in voice, offering in words the feeling of an era before. Consider these passages from *The Singing Wilderness:*

The movement of a canoe is like a reed in the wind. Silence is part of it, and the sounds of lapping water, bird songs, and wind in the trees. It is part of the medium through which it floats, the sky, the water, the shores. . . . There is magic in the feel of a paddle and the movement of a canoe, a magic compounded of distance, adventure, solitude, and peace. The way of a canoe is the way of the wilderness, and of a freedom almost forgotten. It is an antidote to insecurity, the open door to waterways of ages past and a way of life with profound and abiding satisfactions. When a man is part of his canoe, he is part of all that canoes have ever known.

At times on quiet waters one does not speak aloud but only in whispers, for then all noise is sacrilege.

Of all his accolades, coups, and indelible impact, one of Olson's personal favorites was Listening Point, a rugged lump of rock topped with old pines on the southern shore of Burntside Lake near Ely. This was his place to connect with Nature and disconnect with distractions. He built a log cabin—his writing shack—on the property and spent countless hours there. Listening Point is listed on the National Register of Historic Places and is preserved by the Listening Point Foundation. "Everybody has a listening-point somewhere," Olson wrote. "It does not have to be in the north or close to the wilderness, but some place of quiet where the universe can be contemplated with awe."

Olson's view of wilderness connection is something we can all appreciate. Learning to live it brings everything else together. Olson shared as much at a 1965 Sierra Club conference:

I have discovered in a lifetime of traveling in primitive regions, a lifetime of seeing people living in the wilderness and using it, that there is a hard core of wilderness need in everyone, a core that makes its spiritual values a basic human necessity. There is no hiding it. . . . Unless we can preserve places where the endless spiritual needs of man can be fulfilled and nourished, we will destroy our culture and ourselves.

Olson never wavered a moment for what he believed in. He wrote about it with sentiment for places that touched him deeply as a child and became the foundation and guidance for the rest of his life. That alone endeared him to those of us hailing from the Northland. There is something very special in the air around here;

after one invigorating breath, it is an elixir that arouses all other senses and shapes who we are.

But Olson was more than just eloquent prose. He drove change by planting the seeds to make it happen, through lobbies and lectures and a vision that recognized that wilderness is a place, an entity, and a spirit.

HIS LEGACY

Up early on a cold winter morning, Sigurd Olson poked a simple thought at his typewriter's keys: *A New Adventure is coming up and I'm sure it will be a good one.*

He died later that day of a heart attack while snowshoeing near a skinny creek not far from his home. After 60 years of conservation activism, Olson was gone. A sad day to be sure, but although not here in physical form, for those of us imbued with his connection to Nature, it's like he never left. Thanks to his unflagging dedication, Minnesota's Boundary Waters Canoe Area Wilderness, the most visited wilderness area in the United States, exists with full federal protection and contains the country's most culturally and ecologically significant lands. Neighboring Voyageurs National Park holds equal reverence and is here largely due to Sigurd Olson.

Northland College, one of his alma maters, established the Sigurd Olson Environmental Institute in his honor. In addition to serving as a central campus education hub, the institute is a leader in conservation efforts throughout the Upper Midwest and works diligently in teaching and inspiring our future conservation leaders.

Olson's verve remains alive and well in northern Minnesota, as well, where a new generation of conservationists and related on-the-ground projects, from ecosystem integrity to habitat loss, carry on his legacy. His namesake Listening Point Foundation tends to his lakeshore getaway and offers educational programs and community events. Every year, hundreds of Olson-inspired voyageurs travel to Listening Point—to hear what's out there and, more importantly, what's inside.

"Without love of the land, conservation lacks meaning or purpose, for only in a deep and inherent feeling for the land can there be dedication in preserving it."

RACHEL CARSON
1907–1964

It is a wholesome and necessary thing for us to turn again to the earth and in the contemplation of her beauties to know the sense of wonder and humility.

RACHEL CARSON WAS BORN IN THE SIGHT OF WATER, IN A SMALL, square white house on a hillside in the middle of a 65-acre farm less than a mile from a gentle curve of the Allegheny River. A squiggly little tributary creek ran between, through forests packed with centuries-old trees and critters and mystery. Rachel Carson ran around in that glorious playground, chasing frogs, floating

97

sticks down the creek, turning up rocks to see what was under them and learning, feeling what Nature is all about.

A decade-plus later, she kept company with the albatross and whales, the sea turtles and fishes. How did she get from the woods and streams to ocean realms? In essence, it started on paper. Something stirred in that young mind as she tapped a natural talent for writing. She shared her adventures, winning first prize for a story appearing in *St. Nicholas* magazine (the same publication showcasing the earliest work of Faulkner and Fitzgerald). Carson graduated high school with honors and earned a scholarship to Pennsylvania College for Women (today's Chatham University), set on an English major and career as a teacher and writer. But like many bright-eyed, vacillating college students, she changed majors halfway through, choosing biology—one of only five women in the program.

"Mr. Chairman, I appreciate the opportunity to discuss with you this morning the problems of environmental hazards and the control of pesticides. The contamination of the environment with harmful substances is one of the major problems of modern life. The world of air and water and soil supports not only the hundreds of thousands of species of animals and plants, it supports man himself. In the past we have often chosen to ignore this fact. Now we are receiving sharp reminders that our heedless and destructive acts enter into the vast cycles of the earth and in time return to bring hazard to ourselves." (From Carson's 1963 statement to Congress regarding the use of DDT)

Carson swiftly earned a summer fellowship at the Woods Hole Marine Biological Laboratory in Massachusetts, providing her first up-close experience with ocean life, and graduated magna cum laude in 1929. Topping it all off was another scholarship, this time from Johns Hopkins University where she earned a masters in zoology, an unheard-of accomplishment for a woman in that era. Prior to graduation, she studied and worked in genetic research with Raymond Perl's Institute for Biological Research, a position that provided the foundation for an extraordinary future.

A dearth of funds put the brakes on her PhD track and she dropped out of grad school in 1934, but it slowed her down only for a moment. She had started writing conservation-based newspaper and magazine articles that caught the attention of the US Bureau of Fisheries. A former professor and mentor encouraged Carson to take the bureau's civil service exam, and she accepted a part-time position there as junior aquatic biologist the next year, excelling immediately. She was quickly nominated to write a series of short radio programs for the bureau's "Romance Under the Waters" marine life feature.

Fishes and plankton, whales and squids, birds and sea turtles, are all linked by unbreakable ties to certain kinds of water. Whales suddenly appear off the slopes of the coastal banks where the swarms of shrimplike krill are spawning, the whales having come from no one knows where, by no one knows what route.

All the while, she continued publishing stories on the state of Nature's threats and ideas for preservation, gaining a loyal audience following; echoing the likes of Leopold and Muir, Carson didn't shy from voicing concern for "the welfare of the fish as well as that of the fisherman." In 1936, she was promoted to the fisheries bureau's newest aquatic biologist (one of only two women in professional roles at the time). Realizing childhood dreams, her earliest assignments occupied space along the shores and on the waters of Chesapeake Bay, interviewing salty ship captains, fishing boat deckhands, and conservation organizations to learn the area's culture and Nature's place in it.

In the heat of World War II, Carson's impact swelled further with research of the underwater world's mysterious, fascinating life, sounds, and topography to assist the US Navy's development of submarine detection equipment. Around this time, it was discovered that DDT, first introduced in 1874, made a powerful insecticide, thus launching a ubiquitous campaign of its "benefits" to the food and agriculture industries. Carson, however, was aware of DDT's downsides; the chemical reared its ugly head in her ocean studies, spawning a battle between scientist and scourge that would soon alter history.

Carson's career trajectory continued at a rapid pace; by now she was firmly entrenched in the ecology realm, complementing it with a rare talent and finesse to present complex scientific data with a lyrical flair that engaged both layman and learned audiences. To wit: *Under the Sea-Wind*, Carson's first book, follows a prior article of the same name and immerses readers in sea life of the Atlantic coast, revealing its intricacies to many people for the first time. It was within these pages that Carson's talent shined for tapping the intrinsic connections of Nature, community, and habitat, as well as the swelling chasm between them and mankind. Her prose in the book's stories, mimicked countless times since, personifies a cast of sea life characters that captivates and appeals to all readers. One of Carson's colleagues commented that her work "turned the subject of the sea to a respectable reading matter for the clientele of the *New Yorker* and *Reader's Digest.*"

Coinciding with the publication of *Sea-Wind*, the Department of the Interior absorbed the Bureau of Fisheries in the formation of the brand new US Fish and Wildlife Service (USFWS), and Carson was immediately hired as a staff aquatic biologist, and while continuing groundbreaking scientific study she churned out bulletins and pamphlets for the general public, including "Conservation in Action," introducing readers to national wildlife refuges, and "Food From the Sea," celebrating the benefits of a seafood diet. She soon became editor-in-chief of all USFWS publications, speechwriting for staff and penning speeches and other documents for congressional testimony.

"The problem you have chosen to explore is one that must be resolved in our time. Contamination of various kinds has now invaded all of the physical environment that supports us—water, soil, air, and vegetation. It has even penetrated that internal environment within the bodies of animals and of men."

Carson also pitched an article on DDT to *Reader's Digest*, whose editors turned it down ("too unpleasant" and doomsday for readers) but she was nonplussed. Years of marine studies at the Bureau of Fisheries and USFWS armed her with stacks of proven data on DDT's effects on animals, especially marine life, and subsequent threat to the environment in general. In tune with the dangers of chemical pesticides and the agricultural industry's love affair with them, Carson could not sit idly by.

"The human race is challenged more than ever before to demonstrate our mastery, not over nature but of ourselves." (Excerpt from a 1963 *CBS Reports* interview with Carson)

By this time, Carson had published a second book, *The Sea Around Us*, a big hit that would see long bestseller tenure, the National Book Award for Nonfiction, a movie version, and sufficient success to allow her to resign from the formal career world and devote herself full time to writing. Her next book, *The Edge of the Sea*, rounded out her trio and helped shape the nascent field of ecology.

While *The Sea Around Us* enjoyed big screen success, Carson continued tidal life research along the Atlantic coast, culminating in a pivotal paper delivered to the American Association for the Advancement of Science and—wouldn't you know it—her concern for and early warnings about the scourge of chemicals played out in real time all over the country.

THE GREAT BALD

Bald eagles are not really bald, of course. The old English word *balde*, meaning white, was given to these regal raptors to match their heads' white feathers. For decades, bald eagles were "sport hunting" targets. Then along came DDT and other poisons that weakened their eggshells, limiting reproduction, and driving the bird to the brink of extinction. Banning of DDT helped launch the eagle to an extraordinary rebound and, thanks to a veto of Ben Franklin's choice of the wild turkey for our nation's symbol, the bald now holds that lofty seat.

The USDA was in the habit of using airplanes to spray fuel oil laced with toxic chemicals over areas of private land to "eliminate" mosquitoes and Dutch elm disease. (Mosquitoes can never be defeated, and Dutch elm killed millions of trees anyway and still preys.) In the Great Fire Ant Controversy, USDA again sprayed untold tons of chemicals over southern states to protect the defenseless public. Problem is, the chemicals essentially killed everything else except the ants; Carson admonished USDA's decisions as "the agricultural equivalent of the atomic bomb." The wake of destruction was clear. Nuclear isotopes are found in baby teeth. Evidence of throat cancer in rats is linked to cranberries doused with toxic insecticide. (This particular event had a positive side in exposing inadequate chemical industry regulation.) A floating mat of household garbage and other debris in Ohio's Cuyahoga River caught fire in 1969, a decades-long poster child for rampant chemical contamination. A New York chemical company with a storied history of dumping toxic chemicals was the culprit in widespread illness among area residents.

In the midst of it all, Carson finished another book project. If her first titles were celebrations and teachings of the natural world, her last woke up the world to an appallingly apathetic sentiment toward other life forms. In a departure from flowing prose about ocean life, *Silent Spring* brought out Carson's understated wrath toward the pesticide plague and the industry provoking it. Naturally, the book enraged pesticide and other chemical corporations, which aimed all their frustrations directly at Carson, discrediting her information, calling her out as a charlatan, and scrambling to reposition themselves to the public as friend, not foe.

Interestingly, the chemical industry was instantly defensive and quick to blame Carson for instigating a ban on their product, but her argument's thrust simply urged more thorough research regarding safe use of existing pesticides and an alternative to DDT. Fortunately, the public melee lit a fire in the federal government and a top-to-bottom investigation of its own policies. Carson testified before a congressional committee and, in the end, DDT was banned, America started caring about Nature, and the modern environmental movement was underway.

By the close of the 1980s, more than 60 percent of the nation viewed the chemical industry as a polluting nuisance or altogether non-essential. And they weren't afraid to speak their mind—letters from fuming citizens, many affiliated with the Committee Against Mass Poisoning, poured into newspapers, sharing disturbing stories of dying birds, wilting vegetable gardens, or simply spouting off and demanding action. The committee captured the nation's attention with a lawsuit aimed at nonchalant decisions to unload insecticides all over people's homes, and Carson was asked to write the story.

She accepted, seeing an opportunity to write directly on environmental destruction and communicate the largely unknown atrocity of biological magnification, the movement of toxic substances up the food chain that increases in concentration with each step.

We poison the gnats in a lake and the poison travels from link to link of the food chain and soon the birds of the lake margins become its victims. We spray our elms and the following springs are silent of robin song, not because we sprayed the robins directly but because the poison traveled, step by step, through the now familiar elm–leaf–earthworm cycle. These are matters of record, observable, part of the visible world around us. They reflect the web of life—or death—that scientists know as ecology. (Silent Spring)

"When we review the history of mankind in relation to the earth we cannot help feeling somewhat discouraged, for that history is for the most part that of the blind or short-sighted despoiling of the soil, forests, waters and all the rest of the earth's resources. We have acquired technical skills on a scale undreamed of even a generation ago. We can do dramatic things and we can do them quickly; by the time damaging side effects are apparent it is often too late, or impossible, to reverse our actions. In attempting to assess the role of pesticides, people too often assume that these chemicals are being introduced into a simple, easily controlled environment, as in a laboratory experiment. This, of course, is far from true."

In light of environmental catastrophe already happening or in the making, Carson's warnings were spot on and, as is often the case with environmental concern, unheeded. We can throw darts at any natural resources–related focus area and find a glaring issue. Especially concerning these days is ice and water, specifically melting of the former and polluting the latter. Glaciers are disappearing; polar ice caps are turning to liquid in state-size chunks; permafrost is losing its perma; and the world's oceans are being slaughtered by plastic, toxic chemicals, overfishing, and a general throwaway attitude. Carson sums it up thusly: "But man is a part of Nature, and his war against Nature is inevitably a war against himself."

"Underlying all of these problems of introducing contamination into our world is the question of moral responsibility, responsibility not only to our own generation but to those of the future." (*Lost Woods: The Discovered Writing of Rachel Carson*)

"To live on the land, we must learn from the sea," says a John Denver lyric about Jacques Cousteau, one of Carson's counterparts and herald of the meaning, and fragility, of our oceans. And yet here we are, biting the hand that feeds us, taking it for granted, apparently with no idea (or desire) to reach an amicable relationship. In her work, Carson spells out that Nature and all of its ingredients are related to everything else, but mankind still doesn't appreciate what's at stake—an emaciated version of Nature or its absence means we don't get to be here either. Overly dramatic? Nope. Look out the window or take a walk; the story is evolving right in front of us. With this tale, however, we have an opportunity and means to craft a favorable ending. We can continue bumbling about, looking no further than the ends of our noses, tiny lifespans, and temporary bank accounts; or stand *with* animals and forests and oceans rather than above it all.

"It is a curious situation that the sea, from which life first arose should now be threatened by the activities of one form of that life. But the sea, though changed in a sinister way, will continue to exist; the threat is rather to life itself." (*The Sea Around Us*)

Rachel Carson died of cancer far too young but never wavered in a belief that an ending with promise is possible, even attainable. While her health faded with sickness, her vision remained clear, with one particular idea for a book that circled back to marked changes to her beloved sea. "In our own lifetime we are witnessing a startling alteration of climate."

Yes, Rachel, we are. And we can make a difference, as you did, if we keep the sea around us.

HER LEGACY

"Only within the moment of time represented by the present century has one species—man—acquired significant power to alter the nature of the world."

Is there a "right" way to remember Rachel Carson? *Silent Spring* became her hallmark and the catalyst igniting a powerful global conservation movement. America banned DDT and woke up to the dangers of unleashing toxic chemicals at will. Her work inspired the Wilderness Act, National Environmental Policy Act, Environmental Protection Agency, Clean Water Act, and Endangered Species Act.

She earned a veritable trophy case of awards, including the John Burroughs Medal (Nature writing's highest honor), New York Zoological Society Gold Medal, Henry Grier Bryant Gold Medal, election to the American Academy of Arts and Letters, and a Simon Guggenheim Fellowship for tidal coast research. The USFWS honored her with the Rachel Carson National Wildlife Refuge, the Sierra Club has a Rachel Carson Society, and a new kinship of contemporary writers carry on her legacy, from Terry Tempest Williams and Theo Colborn to Annie Dillard and Bill Bryson. Many of them also boast on-the-ground scientific chops, track records of political wrangling, and efforts supporting global climate issues.

That kind of influence is an impressive legacy to be sure, with a direct impact on Nature every step of the way, but there was more to Rachel Carson. With such visible mainstream buzz for

Silent Spring, it can be easy to forget she was a highly respected marine biologist and prolific writer of engaging prose filled at once with professorial knowledge and poetic wonder.

"Those who dwell among the beauties and mysteries of the earth are never alone or weary of life."

The prevailing message in her words and actions is an awareness of Nature's fragile foundation, that what we have with us today—brooding, bulwark mountain ranges, endless miles of desert sands, ocean fathoms filled with mystery and knowledge and life—seems "forever" but is, in fact, as delicate as butterfly wings.

Carson taught us we cannot indiscriminately flog our environment and its wild residents without a reckoning and in many respects, both are in worse shape than ever. She also reminds us that if we don't tinker too much with Nature's habits, we reap what is "infinitely healing in the repeated refrains of Nature, the assurance that dawn comes after night, and spring after winter."

We stand now where two roads diverge. But unlike the roads in Robert Frost's familiar poem, they are not equally fair. The road we have long been traveling is deceptively easy, a smooth superhighway on which we progress with great speed, but at its end lies disaster. The other fork of the road—the one less traveled by—offers our last, our only chance to reach a destination that assures the preservation of the earth.

EDWARD ABBEY

1927–1989

KIRK MCKOY/CONTRIBUTOR/LOS ANGELES TIMES/©GETTY IMAGES

The love of wilderness is more than a hunger for what is always beyond reach; it is also an expression of loyalty to the earth, the earth which bore us and sustains us, the only paradise we shall ever know, the only paradise we ever need, if only we had the eyes to see.

AN EMPTY SCHLITZ CAN (OR BUDWEISER—PROBABLY BOTH) sailed out the car window, fermenting the turbulent air for an instant, performing a couple of terribly executed pirouettes and tinking on the cracked pavement like an out of tune xylophone before finally rolling to a stop next to a stubby mesquite bush. A blight on the highway? Not according to Ed. "Littering the public highway? Of course, I litter the public highway. Every chance I get. After all, it's not the beer cans that are ugly; it's the highway that is ugly."

Edward Abbey didn't like highways (but contradicted that sentiment by driving on them, as little as possible if he could help it) and was quick to point out that paved roads are essentially blackened tongues of destruction. He saw it firsthand in those easygoing late 1950s days, working as a park ranger at a remote outpost in Utah's Arches National Monument (now a national park). The outpost was at the far end of a long, rutted, washboard dirt road, secluded, quiet, and utterly devoid of other humans— just the way Abbey liked it. A little trailer served as housing, and he enjoyed sitting out front near a scraggly juniper long after sundown, just him and the desert. All was right with the world until, "It was then that I heard the discordant note, the snarling whine of a jeep in low range and four-wheel drive."

The jeep contained a few Bureau of Land Management workers and survey equipment; a brand-new road was coming to the park, the workers said. You'll have thirty times as many tourists in here. Abbey cringed; later, some carefully planted survey stakes were mysteriously relocated. He knew lots of vehicles meant lots of people, a death knell to wilderness and solitude, both with which he was hopelessly enamored and protective against ill treatment.

The new road opened the floodgates; visitors poured into Arches (visitor numbers at Arches today top 1.5 million) and scores of other previously peaceful lands in the West, obliterating what Abbey, Cactus Ed, held closest to heart. His outpost and its solitude are long gone, with similar stories evolving all over the country. Abbey freely shared his opinion on this disturbing trend: "No more cars in national parks. Let the people walk. Or ride horses, bicycles, mules, wild pigs—anything—but keep the automobiles and the motorcycles and all their motorized relatives out. We have agreed not to drive our automobiles into cathedrals, concert halls, art museums, legislative assemblies, private bedrooms, and the other sanctums of our culture; we should treat our national parks with the same deference, for they, too, are holy places. An increasingly pagan and hedonistic people (thank God!), we are learning finally that the forests and mountains and desert canyons are holier than our churches. Therefore, let us behave accordingly."

Abbey did not intend to be an activist or environmentalist, but he was of the same cloth in a fierce determination to defend what he loved, typically doing so with dry wit humility. "Saving the world is only a hobby. Most of the time I do nothing." He didn't see himself as a naturalist or Nature writer, either; he chose novelist, with a life goal to write a "fat masterpiece." "The only birds I can recognize without hesitation are the turkey vulture, fried chicken, and the rosy-bottomed skinny-dipper. I'll never make it as a naturalist. If a label is required say that I am one who loves unfenced country."

"I thought of the wilderness we had left behind us, open to sea and sky, joyous in its plenitude and simplicity, perfect yet vulnerable, unaware of what is coming, defended by nothing, guarded by no one." (*Beyond the Wall: Essays from the Outside*)

Abbey's pilgrimage to open country began on America's other side. He was born and raised in oddly named Indiana, Pennsylvania, a quiet, hilly, wooded place at the time. His family moved around the East, sometimes in campsites, other times in New Jersey. His father inspired Abbey's ideals of the great big world to the west and, with the prospect of the war draft looming after high school, he left home to explore, heading that way on foot, hitchhiking on empty freight train cars when available. With his first step into the Southwest, he was instantly smitten by its desert crags, vast emptiness, and solitude. "I felt I was getting close to the West of my deepest imaginings—the place where the tangible and the mythical became the same." He had found his place and, when asked later in his fabled career, would tell you as such: "My home is the American West. All of it."

> "Standing there, gaping at this monstrous and inhumane spectacle of rock and cloud and sky and space, I feel a ridiculous greed and possessiveness come over me. I want to know it all, possess it all, embrace the entire scene intimately, deeply, totally." (*Desert Solitaire*)

Before settling into that home, however, Abbey enlisted in the US Army, spending two years as a military police officer in Italy. He was promoted twice but, never much good at following protocol, was subsequently *de*moted (twice, refusing to salute) and honorably discharged. The entire experience, in fact, was mostly about chasing girls around town, getting drunk on sunny afternoons, and nurturing a growing distaste for big government and regulations.

Military tenure was a boon in the long run, providing the means to study philosophy at the University of New Mexico. As an undergraduate, Abbey was editor of the student newspaper, a post from which he was soon fired for printing an unsavory cover quote. He shrugged it off and earned bachelor's and master's degrees by 1956, celebrating by traveling with his first wife to Edinburgh, Scotland, to teach at the university and then back to Stanford University on a creative writing fellowship. That year also saw the release of his first novel, *Jonathan Troy*, followed closely by *The Brave Cowboy*, which evolved into the movie *Lonely Are the Brave*, shot in New Mexico with Kirk Douglas in the starring and production roles.

ART IN MOTION

Arches National Park boasts well over 2,000 natural stone arches, more than anywhere on Earth, thanks to extreme temperatures and nature's eternal, creative artistry of wind and water. Balanced Rock, for example, is a park highlight; a 3,600-ton Easter egg–shaped boulder impossibly perched on a sandstone dais. This exquisite land is under constant threat of oil and gas drilling and, like all of our remaining natural wonders, needs equally persistent defense.

Movie rights were an amusing but temporary aside, not impressing Abbey all that much, but things got interesting in the late 1960s with *Desert Solitaire*, his first nonfiction work that he said wasn't published as much as "released from its cage and turned loose upon an unsuspecting public."

It started, naturally, in the desert. During Abbey's ranger years at Arches, his love of the wilderness West coalesced with utter disgust of a scourge of park "improvements" and laundry list of fatuous decisions from Washington. Whether he already had an innate vision or the steady trickle of danger fueled the perspective, Abbey could see what was coming, what was already happening to Nature's wild places; he called out oil and power companies and government for distorting truths and bamboozling the public into believing burning fossil fuels wasn't so bad. More than 40 years ago he advocated for phasing out the auto industry monolith and replacing it with trains, buses, and bicycles—an idea then thought to be preposterous, but if even partially implemented would have by now drastically reduced the emissions and climate change shackles we are handing over to our children.

Abbey despised dams, corporate greed, governmental bumbling, and overpopulation. Environmentalism wasn't a thing at the time of his earlier writing, but *Solitaire*'s timing hit a bull's-eye. Its

1968 publication coincided with a nation gripped in the clutches of the Vietnam War, horrific assassinations of King and Kennedy, and riots and other civil unrest. Topping it off were similar environmental atrocities—think pesticide poisoning in the millions of tons, air and water putrid with pollution, confetti of litter splattered over highways, unchecked razing of forests . . . the list goes on.

Abbey had long tired of the carnage, inaction by those behind desks of supposed power, and attendance of undesirable insolence creeping among the American people. "Society is like a stew. If you don't stir it up every once in a while then a layer of scum floats to the top." Fans of *The Monkey Wrench Gang* will recognize a similar sentiment:

One man alone can be pretty dumb sometimes, but for real bona fide stupidity, there ain't nothin' can beat teamwork.

At the time, Abbey was riding out his own wave of angst, a touch frustrated with writing and women and a dusting of other ails. One such prickly matter came along in 1962 with the publication of *Fire on the Mountain*, where an ornery, land-hardened western rancher butts heads with a meddling government. I particularly enjoyed the book, but public reception at the time was tepid. The same year, *Silent Spring* happened. Rachel Carson outed abhorrent risks and aftermaths of pesticide use, specifically DDT's devastation to wild birds and the introduction of biological magnification. The book galvanized the nation's views on environment and inspired federal regulations still in effect today.

Quite a disparity between books, to be sure, and likely part of Abbey's impetus to sit down and tally up how much money he had made as a writer so far. The grand total was just shy of $13,000 for 10 years' hard labor.

Desert Solitaire changed Abbey's lyrical landscape and plowed into millions of readers' lives. The book extolls his thoughts, experiences, and blunt opinions about the Desert Southwest, with just enough scientific fact (and folly) to educate while infusing a touch of Thoreau, Muirisms, and laugh out loud humor. He is simultaneously melancholy and cynical (calling the book a "eulogy") and, in the process, created an immediate legion of mainstream fans. Abbey gave us a new perspective on Nature that didn't leave out things that stung a little.

Two years after *Solitaire's* release, the country celebrated its first Earth Day and Abbey's stories about the desert rocketed to cult classic status, becoming required backpack fodder and one of American literature's most revered Nature narratives. Abbey himself, however, didn't always understand peoples' fascination with reading about the outdoors when "it's more interesting simply to go for a walk into the heart of it." He was more intrigued by the perpetual struggle between anthropocentric views and a balanced (sensible) relationship with Nature. As such, his writing, and attitude, sometimes carried abrasive tones, but he took no bullshit when it came to what truly mattered. "I write in a deliberately provocative and outrageous manner because I like to startle people. I have no desire to simply soothe or please. I would rather risk making people angry than putting them to sleep. It's hard for me to stay serious for more than half a page at a time." He never held back in his work and believed it an inherent charge of writers to tell the truth—"especially unpopular truth. Especially truth that offends the powerful, the rich, the well-established, the traditional, the mythic." He may have best summarized his philosophy when he wrote: "Better a cruel truth than a comfortable delusion."

This related passage from *Desert Solitaire* conveys Abbey's views on wilderness and its constant gut punches from the human population:

Wilderness is not a luxury but a necessity of the human spirit, and as vital to our lives as water and good bread. Growth for the sake of growth is the ideology of the cancer cell. A patriot must always be ready to defend his country against his government.

Roughly a decade later, he was right there at the start of the militant conservation movement with a new novel about a group of merry, disorganized pranksters drifting around desert country, instigating skirmishes in the name of conservation—The Monkey Wrench Gang, with a decisive, resounding goal of blowing up Glen Canyon Dam (the same one that created Lake Powell, obliterated millennia-carved canyons, derailed Abbey's favorite rafting trip, and really pissed him off). More comedy than anything, the book was satire to some and a property destruction how-to guide for others. The gang in the story didn't accomplish their goal, but Abbey unintentionally set the stage for a little civil unrest.

At the heart of it, however, we can see what drives the author's words. "A civilization which destroys what little remains of the wild, the spare, the original, is cutting itself off from its origins and betraying the principle of civilization itself."

If wilderness is outlawed, only outlaws can save wilderness.

His candid opinion of Lake Powell:

Lake Powell: storage pond, silt trap, evaporation tank and garbage dispose-all, a 180-mile-long incipient sewage lagoon.

Some environmentalist camps decided it was time for a dedicated group to lead the movement, thus, Earth First! was born. Members of the radical environmental advocacy group protested in animal costumes, marched with signs to the Capitol, and sometimes took part in eco-sabotage, from dumping sugar into bulldozer gas tanks to spiking trees—monkey wrenching. The group is still active today, sporting a monkey wrench logo and holding Abbey in high esteem. But in those early, bristly years,

Abbey knew that, far from a simple endeavor, wilderness preservation would forever be a battle. He had seen and intimately
mingled with Arches (National Moneymint, as he called it) before
the paved roads, hiked and floated Glen Canyon before it disap-
peared. He walked in solitude with cactus and cliffrose; flirted
with calamity in skinny, hidden canyons; and floated naked in
cold mountain streams. In his own lifetime, all of that was essentially lost because of the obdurate spread of overpopulation and
"improvements" to Nature's original guise.

What was Ed Abbey like in the wild? I found out in my
heady college years. (Didn't meet him in person but the next best
thing.) I traded a statistics class for Nature writing and shortly
into the semester we were reading Abbey. Better yet, my professor
later shared some inside scoop on that night he spent drinking
with Ed in Durango.

A small town with a cowboy-rancher-mountain hippie vibe
at the time, Durango hosted a Western Literature Association
(WLA) conference. Abbey was on the guest list, and another
publishing luminary, a friend of Ed's, arrived early and stopped at
his rental house prior to the event, my professor in tow.

The first look at Abbey was long, in the physical sense. He
was sitting way back in a puffy recliner with legs stretched out so
far they seemed to reach the other side of the room. He unfolded
from the chair and stood up for a handshake, a tall and lean bloke,
somewhat grumpy but maybe just the quiet sort, with a tough-to-
break veneer. After the conference, Abbey softened and escorted
the college English professor to the Strater Hotel, where they
secured a booth along a wall and enjoyed a few brews.

Sometime during the evening, Abbey confided he was sorry
he wrote *Desert Solitaire*. He felt he betrayed the cause and the
Southwest because now too many people went there and too
many people ruin just about everything. Well, what about *The
Monkey Wrench Gang*? Turns out he wrote that one mainly to
include his friend and naturalist Doug Peacock. (Peacock was

inspiration for the book's feisty main character, George Washington Hayduke.) Abbey certainly did not intend to start a movement with the story, and it bothered him more than many people realize. People kept asking him to attend activist events like the Glen Canyon Dam "crack" unveiling, but Abbey instead became more reclusive.

He loved the outdoors, wholly and unconditionally, and was far more content immersing in it than most anything else. Even on rare days when others joined him, Abbey kept to himself. "Most of my wandering in the desert I've done alone. Not so much from choice as from necessity. I generally prefer to go into places where no one else wants to go. I find that in contemplating the natural world my pleasure is greater if there are not too many others contemplating it with me, at the same time."

On a hike in southern Utah's Grand Gulch, an offshoot of the Grand Canyon, he loped along quietly, pointing out things of interest—historical, mostly, and infrequently. After a couple of hours, it got even quieter; someone would point out, say, a sheep on the canyon rim and Abbey would simply nod. None of the group said much. It was like a hushed church service, each person enjoying the experience on their own terms.

"There are some good things to be said about walking. Not many, but some. Walking takes longer, for example, than any other known form of locomotion except crawling. Life is already too short to waste on speed. I have a friend who's always in a hurry; he never gets anywhere. To be everywhere at once is to be nowhere forever, if you ask me.

"My most memorable hikes can be classified as 'Shortcuts that Backfired.'"

At another Western Lit conference in Albuquerque, the professor brought along a grad student for thesis study or some such activity. "There's Abbey right over there. Would you like to meet him?" The grad student nearly shrieked in delight, shaking his hand and babbling about how she had read all his books, biggest fan, so wonderful to meet you. She told him she was especially fond of *The Monkey Wrench Gang* and wanted to know more about it. Abbey turned to the prof and said, "Doc, did I write that piece of shit?"

Abbey was always interested in whatever he was working on right now. For example, he tired of people clamoring on about his more well-known titles when they were missing great stuff in *Slumgullion Stew*. A vicious cycle, for lack of better words, culminating in a way at yet another WLA meeting in Denver, where Abbey would receive a lifetime achievement award to hang on his wall, much fanfare and the like. Ed, of course, wasn't thrilled and said he couldn't make it, that he was going to Mexico. That's odd, thought those close to him; he hates Mexico. He didn't make it to Mexico, and his comment was more a verbal desire to escape. A couple of weeks later, Abbey died.

Ed Abbey made us truly look at a place, whatever and wherever it may be. Places we live, visit, dream about. He made us look and feel with "all of our senses," the best way to tune in to Nature. He wanted to be close to the West, from his first step into it and after his last, buried somewhere in the desert. His request upon death: He wanted his body transported in the bed of a pickup truck. He wanted to be buried as soon as possible. He wanted no undertakers. No embalming, for Godsake. No coffin. Just an old sleeping bag . . . Disregard all state laws concerning burial. "I want my body to help fertilize the growth of a cactus or cliff rose or sagebrush or tree." At the graveside ceremony, he wanted gunfire and a little music. "No formal speeches desired, though the deceased will not interfere if someone feels the urge. But keep it all simple and brief." He wanted a big, raucous wake with more music, and bagpipes. "And a flood of beer and booze! Lots of singing, dancing, talking, hollering, laughing, and lovemaking."

At the end of a long, raggedy dirt road in Arizona's Cabeza Prieta Desert, a crooked headstone includes Abbey's name, birth and death years, and his parting words:

NO COMMENT

HIS LEGACY

"The idea of wilderness needs no defense, it only needs defenders."

Cactus Ed is buried in The Big Empty. Exactly where he wanted to be. Before landing there, however, he gave conservation a powerful place in the tumultuous 60s and 70s and became a cult hero to a population of souls desperate for direction. His writing was infused with passion and his tetchy personality offended or inspired, whether intended or not. Most evident and victorious for Nature was governmental action that set aside millions of acres of wilderness, cleaned up filthy river pollution, and halted construction of dams that weren't needed in the first place.

"The most common form of terrorism in the U.S.A. is that carried on by bulldozers and chainsaws. It is not enough to understand the natural world; the point is to defend and preserve it. Sentiment without action is the ruin of the soul."

There is plenty of reason to be gloomy these days, what with the omen of oil drilling from the Arctic to the Gulf, destructive weather events, soaring global temperatures, and much more. Environmentalists today are saddled with an increasingly technological and impersonal world struggling to stay in contact with roots inexorably linked to the oceans and forests and soil below its feet. Abbey said we need balance. "Balance, that's the secret. Moderate extremism. The best of both worlds."

He does not altogether discount cities because they are "the essence and substance of us all," but he urged (demanded) we all wake up and use a little self-control with wilderness, refrain from destroying every inch of it, and remain vigilant for further human bumbling. Today's environmentalism (thankfully) has adopted a conscious awareness of stewardship, due in large part to dramatic climate change, and more people realize the world was not made by nor should it be ruled by us.

Abbey saw human influence on Nature through a different lens and realized its inevitable effect long before today's pervasive, fancy scientific talk. I think he'd be proud, in his own roundabout way, to have fueled a new generation of conservation crusaders when we need them most.

"Be as I am—a reluctant enthusiast. . . . a part-time crusader, a half-hearted fanatic. Save the other half of yourselves and your lives for pleasure and adventure. It is not enough to fight for the land; it is even more important to enjoy it. While you can. While it's still here. So get out there and hunt and fish and mess around with your friends, ramble out yonder and explore the forests, climb the mountains, bag the peaks, run the rivers, breathe deep of that yet sweet and lucid air, sit quietly for a while and contemplate the precious stillness, the lovely, mysterious, and awesome space. Enjoy yourselves, keep your brain in your head and your head firmly attached to the body, the body active and alive, and I promise you this much; I promise you this one sweet victory over our enemies, over those desk-bound men and women with their hearts in a safe deposit box, and their eyes hypnotized by desk calculators. I promise you this; You will outlive the bastards.

"Simply because humankind have the power now to meddle or 'manage' or 'exercise stewardship' in every nook and cranny of the world, does not mean that we have a right to do so. Even less, the obligation."

WILL STEGER
1944–

You can be brilliant in mathematics or with computers, with great prospects on Wall Street or in Silicon Valley, but unless you understand the interdependency of the environment where we live, the planet is doomed. We can decide our fate only if we fully understand the consequences of our action.

REMEMBER WHEN WE WERE KIDS AND DREAMED ABOUT THE North Pole, especially at Christmas time, and what it must be like up there covered in snow and icebergs? Will Steger did, too, but when he grew up he put on a warm jacket, hitched to a dogsled, and went there.

It started with Huck Finn. Steger grew up with eight siblings in Richfield, Minnesota, just south of the Minneapolis skyline, scurrying about the neighborhood and exploring shadowy woods along the Mississippi River valley. His family didn't pack up and head off to grand outdoor travels all that often, and never camped in the woods, but one day Steger got hold of *Adventures of Huckleberry Finn*, the ultimate young kid tale of vagabond escapades. Floating a raft to parts unknown, barefoot with a straw hat and overalls, chewing on a stalk of wheat—what more could a boy want? Steger was hooked. The book sparked an insatiable explorer spirit and served as a launch pad for one of the world's most renowned and influential conservationists.

Before he donned a parka for the far north, however, a 15-year-old Steger and his brother urged a motorboat into the Mississippi River in Minnesota and went the other way, plying the muddy waters clear to New Orleans in their own Huck Finn escapade. The trip was chock-full of colorful characters, hardscrabble riverside towns, boisterous wildlife, and enchanting scenic sights. It was an arduous venture, as well (they had to repeat the trip upstream to get back home), whetting Steger's appetite for more. Four years later, he teamed with a friend to kayak 3,000 miles across Canada and Alaska, hitchhiking home when they finally stopped paddling.

He dreamed of living in the wilderness in a log cabin, clearing some land for gardens and living a self-sufficient life. Before turning 26, Steger piloted 10,000 kayak miles, including the length of Alaska's Yukon River and Canada's Mackenzie, hitchhiked to hang out in San Francisco, and delved deeper into mystical lands north of his Minnesota home turf.

"Wilderness ignites a sense of power and forges tenacious resolve to harness that power for the good of all."

Destinations and surroundings changed but the outdoors drove Steger ever forward. By age 25, he earned an undergraduate degree in science and a master's in education from the University of St. Thomas in St. Paul and taught middle school science but "after eight or nine years I didn't feel I was reaching enough people." He wanted to share what he learned about the wilderness with a much larger audience and looked to the Arctic for inspiration, specifically a dogsled trip to the North Pole to bring to light its stark beauty and fragility.

By this time, Steger had picked up his city stakes and moved to Ely, a generations-proud outpost town in northern Minnesota and gateway to the Boundary Waters Canoe Area Wilderness. There, he established a winter school leading area students on wilderness trips via skis or dogsleds, the latter which had rapidly become Steger's lifeline. Be it a bag of groceries or expedition equipment, sled dogs whisked it all from the nearest road and years later made possible some of his legendary adventures.

Steger teamed up with friend Paul Schurke, cobbling together a base camp of sorts in Schurke's garage and Steger's log shack, complete with sod roof, in Ely. They built dogsleds by hand in Ely Memorial High School's wood shop; Steger bred his own dogs to pull them; and, in those oh-so-innocent, social media–free days, they raised money selling T-shirts and buttons.

In March of 1986, Steger's team of eight, including Ann Bancroft, also a Minnesota native and a pioneering explorer in her own right, departed Canada's northernmost shore with three tons of supplies and forty-nine plucky dogs leading the way. Fifty-four days later, navigating entirely by sextant, the group wrapped up the first confirmed dogsled journey to the North Pole without outside support or resupply, an otherworldly feat to be sure—accompanied by equally onerous hardships. Steger: "It was so difficult. It was moment to moment all the time. There was a specific time, about 30 days in, that I thought we weren't going to make it. I actually thought I had made a mistake on the logistics."

The route was littered with pressure ridges of ice upwards of 40 feet high, unexpected stretches of open water, and temperatures plummeting to 70 below zero. At one point, Bancroft fell through Arctic Ocean ice and spent the next three days in violent shivers. A camp stove sparked a tent fire, they lost a lead dog, and the sextant broke down. Imagine slogging across millions of square miles of drifting, cracking, growling ice and your navigation tool goes on the fritz. Amazingly, the team disassembled it with a Swiss Army knife and fixed the glitch. After jettisoning gear during a stretch of extremely slow going, they reached the Pole with only a few remaining pounds of food. *National Geographic* magazine chronicled the trip in a cover story later that year, hailing the trek as a "landmark in polar exploration."

"It's such a cliche talking about being in the moment, but it is in that moment when you see the true beauty of everything that's around you."

The Steger International Polar Expedition was among the most successful in history and launched Steger's career as a leading figure in dogsled expeditions, polar environmental issues, Arctic preservation, and climate change. In 1988, Steger completed a 1,600-mile south-to-north traverse of Greenland, the longest unsupported dogsled expedition in history. A year later, he notched the first dogsled traverse of Antarctica on the International Trans-Antarctica Expedition, a seven-month, 3,741-mile trek. Global media coverage of the trip thrust Steger into the climate change limelight, especially in the classroom. Live social media updates and dispatches brought his firsthand, real-time experience to more than fifteen million students and woke up the world to climate change. Steger later noted that, while people at the time realized climate change was a thing, denial is, too, and melting polar icecaps seemed far away and something for experts (or future generations) to worry about. Sadly, even denial won't fix the mess we're in now.

Way back in 1995, Steger showed us a warming planet would bring unprecedented alterations to our environment and lives with the International Arctic Project, the first dogsled traverse of the Arctic Ocean from Russia to Canada's Ellesmere Island. Today, it is no longer possible to replicate Steger's polar expeditions, as untold miles—and, in fact, enormous swaths of ice shelves—have melted or collapsed into the sea. Where once was ice is now open water and the pace of melting is only increasing—Arctic regions are warming faster than anywhere else on Earth. "Almost all the expeditions I did in the polar regions, you can't do anymore. Now you can't reach the pole by dog team ever again because of the water on the Arctic Ocean."

Steger remains adamant and active in efforts to engage audiences with what this means to all life on Earth. He believes international cooperation is the only way to mitigate our already significant damage and losses and hopes continued pressure will drive change. "If we could cut carbon dioxide emissions by 80 percent over the next 20 years we could perhaps prevent this. If we continue burning fossil fuels as we are today in the very near future, the ice shelf will slip into the ocean." Steger's voice and presence in the climate change arena are a place to start; along with presenting at lectures and an array of related appearances, he realizes his time on the ice is powerful evidence we are in a precarious environmental position. "Being a public person gives you a certain amount of power in a way. For myself, it was an opportunity to do education projects. Everything I've done with the climate and the environment, if I wasn't known, I wouldn't be able to do that."

To that end, he established Climate Generation: A Will Steger Legacy (formerly the Will Steger Foundation) in Ely, with headquarters based in Minneapolis. The innovative nonprofit's focus is educating and galvanizing people and communities to

WHITE PINE REDUX

Outside Will Steger's back door is well over one million acres of primeval wilderness—the Quetico Superior. Standing tall for centuries was the noble white pine, until logging decimated all big trees in the north. What's left today is dwindling and at risk of extinction. Disease is one culprit, as well as the usual habitat loss and now an increase in saplings gobbled by deer. The Quetico Superior Foundation's White Pine Initiative works feverishly to plant and care for new trees and revive the Northland's legacy species.

identify opportunities for climate change solutions. Supporting Climate Generation is the wildly popular Steger Wilderness Center in Ely, an idea hatched in a tent in the middle of an Antarctica snowfield. Steger wanted a place that carried on his core values of sustainability and self-sufficiency, instilling confidence and wherewithal to make a difference in today's overwhelming environmental challenges. The Center's mission echoes his original vision, "to create a transformative wilderness experience that will inspire and motivate new discoveries and bold action to improve the world" through responsible land stewardship and the ultimate goal of a sustainable planet.

That's a bold statement, held true through one man's lifelong love of Nature and steadfast dedication to giving back by reimagining solutions and inspiring interdependency with the planet. The Center's physical being exudes as much in its incorporation of wind, solar, biomass, and various other "off the grid" energy sources, as well as locally sourced construction materials. On-site gardens, of course, keep the Center stocked with fresh produce. Close to the land, with just enough modern convenience.

Will Steger's impact in his native Minnesota and, indeed, around the world can hardly be measured on paper. If he cared about a trophy case, it would be heavy with achievements like this: the National Geographic Society's first Explorer-in-Residence and recipient of their John Oliver La Gorce Medal, the Explorer Club's Lowell Thomas and Finn Ronne Memorial Awards, five honorary doctorates (University of St. Thomas, Westminster College, Northland College, Hamline University, Franklin Pierce University), and the Lindbergh Award for his efforts raising awareness of constant environmental threats and highly visible effects of climate change. *National Geographic Adventure* presented Steger a lifetime achievement award for his climate change research and discoveries, and he has gathered with prominent world leaders to discuss and advise on how best to preserve Antarctica.

One riveting example was a ceremony at Mount Rushmore, featuring former president George H. W. Bush. Steger had met Bush face-to-face a few weeks earlier and through a who-you-know network, Steger managed to get a letter about the North Pole expedition in front of the president. It worked—at the ceremony, Bush announced a mining ban in Antarctica as "an important international responsibility" that would "ensure the protection of these natural resources for generations."

Steger also found time during and between expeditions to write four books—*Over the Top of the World*, *Crossing Antarctica*, *North to the Pole*, and *Saving the Earth*.

"I consider it important to challenge myself and do things I couldn't imagine doing a couple years ago."

Only the fourth person in history to reach both the North and South Poles, Will Steger is still at it. From 2015 to 2019, he embarked on four different expeditions, starting with a 300-mile trek across the Boundary Waters Canoe Area Wilderness, Voyageurs National Park, and Quetico Provincial Park. The next year, he hosted the Northwestern Ontario Solo Expedition, 350 miles via lakes and rivers from northern Ontario to Ely. Then he conducted another long journey from Burchell Lake, Ontario, back to his Ely cabin, and 2019's slog across Canada's immense Barren Lands.

We salute your wanderlust, Will, and, more importantly, what you've done with it. Our climate is hemorrhaging but your work is a finger in the leak. Maybe we can pull together and help you plug it for good.

> "It was a great expedition; to be out there alone and in the wilderness, you really get close to yourself and your spirit and your vision get clearer."

HIS LEGACY

> "Having traveled for 45 years in the Arctic, what I've seen the last 15 years is shocking. We need to finally face up that we have an issue here and we need to get back to solutions."

Through a career spanning more than a half-century, Will Steger has led some of history's most definitive polar expeditions and plied nearly 100,000 miles of river and ice in the name of Arctic preservation and climate change awareness. After the horrifying collapse of Antarctica's Larsen B ice shelf in 2002, Steger felt a call to action and left northern Minnesota's wilderness for a houseboat on the Mississippi River, within walking distance of the state capitol, for close access to those in power. He gave more than one hundred presentations on various stages to educate large population bases, sent online videos to show the effect of climate change on their way of life, and continues to focus on inspiring understanding of the deteriorating Arctic, arguably our planet's most pressing emergency situation.

His Wilderness Center offers the ideal stage on which to unite leaders and community residents to brainstorm solutions. Sprouting six stories from Ely's piney woods, the Center, nicknamed the Castle, gleams with a shiny glass atrium, flanked with turrets and stone terraces all clad in locally harvested granite. Green stone for steps was plucked from a ridgeline on the property. From a small balcony at the building's highest reaches, views of forests and lake country unfurl far to the north. More than 25 years in the making, the homegrown sustainability think tank Steger created has upped the ante by establishing a trust to carry on his wilderness legacy.

He believes wholly in the power of wilderness to spark action and that wilderness in spirit and place can empower a new generation of climate drivers through stories and action. Steger saw climate change in its earliest iterations, long before the world at large, long before it became disturbing mainstream news. We weren't ready to talk about climate change yet and most certainly didn't recognize its potential severity. Steger deftly delivered messages from his expeditions and targeted specific issues such as high-altitude Arctic pollution to kindle curiosity, and when the internet came around, fired off word to the masses. Succeeding projects snowballed in complexity, and Steger's voice today booms louder than ever.

After years of political stumping, he eventually returned to his Ely homestead because, after all, that's where his heart is. It's where it all started: an idea for a journey to what matters. "There's not enough beauty in our lives. That's the problem."

Steger wants to change that. "I plan to work with small groups of decision-makers in a wilderness setting so I can help make positive changes that will affect humanity and preserve our precious environment. This will be my legacy."

FIGHTERS

You can't conserve what you haven't got.

—MARJORY STONEMAN DOUGLAS

THE CHARACTERS IN THIS BOOK ARE SLOTTED INTO THINKER, doer, and fighter chapters, but they all have a communal bond—an allegiance to Nature. In some cerebral or corporeal manifestation, they connected so fully with the natural world that it guided their lives through words, deeds, adventures, and defense. Thoreau pondered, Carson inspired a movement, Abbey adored Nature and decried its abuse, Steger showed us the damage and fostered redemption.

While these dedicated conservation luminaries and their brethren wouldn't shy away from standing up for what they believed in, this final selection of conservation crusaders were scrappers, more inclined to gather the townsfolk and instigate a revolution, march onto a stage, and proselytize to a cause or get right up in there and tell it like it is.

First up is a pair of feisty women who backed down to no one in support of species and resource preservation. Rosalie Edge prowled the highbrow New York society scene before transforming into "the most honest, unselfish, indomitable hellcat in the history of conservation," firing the first salvo of environmental activism more than three decades before the demure Rachel

Carson stole the show. Speaking of Carson, Marjory Stoneman Douglas's unrelenting support of Florida's Everglades saw similar impact to *Silent Spring*. She lived to 108 and never for a moment stopped fighting for South Florida's natural treasures.

Die-hard mountaineer David Brower is hailed by many as the father of the modern environmental movement, giving nearly 70 years to staunch activism. Martin Litton was the ultimate river runner, spending more time floating the Colorado than at home, and pioneered river running with wooden dories. He teamed with Brower, Abbey, and other conservation powerhouses in vehement opposition to river dams. Dr. John Francis, nicknamed The Planetwalker, gave up motorized vehicle use for more than two decades and traveled the world on foot to raise environmental awareness. Chico Mendes fought tooth and nail to preserve South American rainforests.

We can look coast to coast, and beyond, and point to places still here, still preserved from efforts of those willing to toe the line with anything that got in the way of the Nature they loved best.

ROSALIE EDGE
1877–1962

PHOTO PROVIDED COURTESY OF HAWK MOUNTAIN SANCTUARY

The time to protect a species is while it is still common.

IN APRIL OF 2018, THE TRUMP ADMINISTRATION GRABBED HOLD
of the Migratory Bird Treaty Act (MBTA) and eviscerated it. The
MBTA was one of America's first environmental laws, passed in
1918, created to prohibit the unregulated killing, capturing, selling, trading, and transport of migratory bird species. As I write
this chapter, more than 100 years have passed with birds traveling
the skies relatively protected from outright murder. In seconds,
Trump's pen became an instrument of doom and changed all that.

Individuals or corporations could now freely kill birds without repercussion, even in the event of catastrophes such as massive oil spills (think 2010's Deepwater Horizon debacle). On an uplifting note, however, prior to this book's publication, a federal court ruling struck down Trump's rollback on wild bird protection, keeping the bird treaty act in place.

If Rosalie Edge could do it, she would have clawed from her Woodlawn Cemetery resting place, marched straight to the White House, snapped Trump's pen in half, and given him a full-on, well-deserved tongue lashing. That was Rosalie's style—plucky and blunt with a stubborn streak a mile long. And, yet, while hers is not generally a household name, she held court for 30 years as one of conservation's loudest voices, widely hailed for her John Muir–like defense of Nature.

Rosalie was born in New York City to a house of means presided over by wealthy British importer John Barrow (first cousin to Charles Dickens), who immersed his daughter in education at the finest private schools and introduced her to the city's high life. Rosalie soon became a regular in the spit-shined socialite crowd, reveling in the scene until age 32 when she married Charles Edge, a well-to-do British chap sitting on a fortune reaped from shipping and railroad dealings. The happy couple traveled for a few years; at a particular stop in Europe, the new Mrs. Edge mingled with leaders of Britain's women's suffrage reform movement. A hint of a flame stirred, erupting to life shortly after she returned to New York City.

During trips to her summer home on the shores of Long Island Sound north of the city, Edge took a strong liking to birds and tagged along with other bird-watchers (hobbyists and respected ornithologists alike) ogling species in Central Park. Edge was hooked and eventually logged more than 800 distinct species in a tattered journal. But then she read an article about the abhorrent slaughter of 70,000 bald eagles in the Alaskan Territory, made worse by the total absence of protest from the public or wildlife protection agencies. Edge learned that, only a few years earlier, Alaska's government was besieged with complaints and (ill-informed) fears from regional farmers and fishermen that eagles were cutting into their take or plucking chickens from barnyards. The "solution" came in the form of bounty laws paying up to two dollars for every eagle eliminated. Kills were verified by cutting feet off dead birds and presenting them to officials.

At the same time, Edge had joined the Equal Franchise Society in the meaty times of women's voting rights and dove headlong into the movement, writing thousands of pro-suffrage articles and pamphlets, giving speeches anywhere and everywhere. She soon secured a seat as secretary-treasurer of New York State's Woman Suffrage Party. She stumped valiantly for women's rights and developed a tenacious resolve for the heated conservation fracas in her future.

In addition to protesting the travesty unfolding in Alaska, Edge wouldn't stand for the then-common practice of killing birds in untold numbers, rare species or not, simply to stuff and mount on a pedestal in a lab somewhere for scientific study. She was also sick and tired of "professional conservationists" meeting clandestinely in back rooms to leverage personal interests and profit margins in selecting which species or wilderness or other natural wonder to save. Corruption was rife and the hands of big timber corporations, the water resources industry, hunting associations, ranchers, chemical companies, and, of course, government officials were all deep in the pockets of groups with allegedly genuine intentions. In fact, one popular and respected wildlife organization essentially prostituted "protected" sanctuaries to hunters for short-term cash influxes, never mind how the animals felt about it.

Edge did not hold a degree from a lofty institution and lacked formal natural resources training or even any applicable on-the-ground experience. She was, however, mentored by some of the country's most respected and accomplished forestry and wildlife leaders, including the likes of Aldo Leopold, Ding Darling, and Bob Marshall. Their tutelage provided Edge the expertise to write on and fight for all manner of conservation issues. Capturing much of her focus were raptor species, forest preservation, dangerous pesticides and other chemicals, and species diversity.

> "I beg each one to keep conservation as his hobby, to keep his independence, his freedom to speak his mind."

By 1929, Edge had had enough of the day's common and disgustingly accepted conservation practice of only preserving species and lands with significant monetary value. She formed the Emergency Conservation Committee (ECC) to make amends. The ECC marched forth in ardent belief of protecting birds and animals of all species *before* they became rare. How about that? Planning ahead with a sound course of action rather than scrambling our way out of knuckleheaded blunders. Edge led the ECC charge from its formation to her final days, coming into her own as an environmental activist and preaching the duty of all people to protect Nature as a rule, not disaster recovery. The ECC drove change and earned clout in conservation arenas. But what was it made of? Aside from one member with tangible conservation experience, the small team had no public members and flew largely under the radar. In a 1980s biography, *A Most Determined Lady: Rosalie Edge, 1877–1962*, written by Edge's son, Peter, we learn the secret:

"Although there were occasionally one or two other members, the Committee was in fact the alter ego of my mother. No wonder its opponents sometimes referred to the 'so-called' Emergency Conservation Committee, or was this revenge for my mother's frequent references to 'so-called' sportsmen? No matter! The Emergency Conservation Committee thrived."

Indeed, the ECC's small stature belied its impact. Its main focus was publishing and distributing news releases, pamphlets, and letters on protection of wildlife species, eventually reaching more than one hundred titles and one million pamphlets circulated. Every ECC mailing inspired editorials in the nation's leading newspapers, catching the public's attention and sparking action. Per Peter Edge: "The ultimate success arose because these appeals and the resulting public support were supplemented by my mother's forthright and extraordinary attitude to people in power, both friends and enemies. An intelligent woman, active and belligerent in the field of conservation—this was a phenomenon with which the men in power, at least fifty years ago, did not know how to cope."

Rosalie Edge was nothing if not persistent, especially in the same ring as heavy-hitter organizations. She accomplished this in large part by cleverly harnessing established judicial processes to call out nefarious or downright illegal goings-on by big-name corporations and conservation groups. Among the most notable coups, Edge went nose-to-nose with the National Audubon Society (then known as the National Association of Audubon Societies), questioning their lackluster protection efforts and habit of ignoring some bird species in favor of others. She attended many Audubon meetings, asking pointed questions often unanswered or altogether avoided by Society leaders, fearing incrimination or exposing ugly truths, such as under-the-table compensation for opening a prized Louisiana sanctuary to muskrat hunters.

Edge butted heads with the Audubon Society for years, underscored with her 1931 lawsuit against the group. Judged in her favor, Edge gained access to roughly 11,000 Society members and led the ECC in promptly informing as many of them as possible of the Society's "lapses in the organization's defense of birds and wildlife." A venomous feud erupted, ultimately leading to the resignation of the Society's then-president T. Gilbert Pearson and a 60 percent drop in membership. Wholesale reorganization

---

MINDING MIGRATION

If you're a fan of raptors, you want to be at Hawk Mountain in autumn for the world's longest-running raptor migration count, active since 1934. In the 4 months from August to December, roughly 18,000 raptors glide through this densely forested mountain region, with some September 1-day peaks of 3,000 birds. Sanctuary staff man lookouts to help identify and count passing avian visitors. Spring migration counts run 45 days in April and May, with around 1,000 birds passing by.

Conservation science studies support migration efforts by promoting a rich mix of habitats including wetlands, streams, forest, and open fields to ensure bird survival and robust future migrations.

---

righted the Audubon ship and directed it toward its place today as one of the world's most respected conservation groups.

The ECC also had tremendous impact on the country's national parks, campaigning to create new parks or augmenting resources for those existing, the crux being enlarging parks with commercially viable virgin forest, not limited solely to scenic benefit. At the time, and still today, proposals to increase park service land ran smack into a contentious wall of resistance from lumber companies, backed by the US Forest Service's credo that forests exist only for economic gain—an unharvested forest is a wasted forest. Congress members from western states vehemently (as they were wont to do) opposed even the slightest hint of interference with timber harvesting. Trees were essentially very tall, log-shaped money.

In a Yellowstone National Park incident, someone in Edge's orbit—could have been a friend, colleague, or random community resident—got their hands on evidence suggesting the park's rangers (on the ground, on-staff federal rangers, no less!) were cruelly mistreating and killing white pelicans within the park. Edge blew up but channeled her anger to return fire by smartly redacting names involved and releasing said evidence to the public, resulting in a good old-fashioned hullabaloo, ranger repercussions, and much-relieved pelicans.

What was next for the socialite-turned-conservation firecracker? Arguably, her crowning achievement originated in the acrid smoke of a gun barrel. Right around 1932, Edge became privy to news of another wildlife bounty genocide happening at a place called Hawk Mountain along a section of the Appalachian Trail in Pennsylvania. Once again, a public tax-funded organization—this time the Pennsylvania Game Commission (PGC)—had initiated a bounty on area avian wildlife. Regional mountains created a wind funnel attracting nearly 100,000 migratory birds every year. Of these species simply making their annual trips south, goshawks somehow stoked the ire of a particular faction of the public. Like a "Wanted" poster nailed to a saloon wall, the PGC rewarded "hunters" or "sportsmen" five dollars for every goshawk shot dead. Mighty gun-wielding warriors could simply stand on the ridgeline and blast away. After all, goshawks were nothing but vermin aloft and had no business cluttering up the state's airspace.

So thought the game commission and its foolhardy followers. But as (bad) luck would have it for those folks, an everyday hiker with a camera snapped some shots of thousands of dead or wounded birds, sharing them with the public and sending shock waves through Pennsylvania's—and the nation's—conservation community. The photos also spurred Edge into action. The slaughter had been occurring for decades, but it would soon come to a screeching halt.

Edge secured a loan to lease (with option to purchase) 1,400 acres on Hawk Mountain, which later ballooned to 2,600 acres, and established Hawk Mountain Sanctuary, the world's first birds of prey sanctuary and America's first citizen-acquired property intended exclusively for conservation purposes. The sanctuary was a huge success with the public and became a model for The Nature Conservancy's future efforts, and migration data from the site helped Rachel Carson verify DDT's link to raptor population decline.

In the end, the guns were silenced on Hawk Mountain and birds fly free to this day. Visitors in the tens of thousands visit every year to view the migration spectacle. Some of the who's-who of celebrity raptors include the bald eagle, American kestrel, northern goshawk, northern harrier, golden eagle, Cooper's hawk, osprey, red-shouldered hawk, and peregrine falcon.

Rosalie Edge hardly stopped to take a breath, continuing to stand up to whatever idiocy brought harm to Nature. She influenced actions of The Wilderness Society, Environmental Defense Fund, and scores of other environmental organizations during a 30-year tenure as the country's most militant—and effective—conservationist. Author Dyana Furmansky penned an appropriate and well-earned salute to this end in her riveting book, *Rosalie Edge, Hawk of Mercy: The Activist Who Saved Nature from the Conservationists*. I highly recommend the read for its engaging history, motivating story, and reminder to never let our guard down.

Despite their enduring and successful work, even our most respected, revered, active conservation organizations must maintain funding for everything from sweeping their office floors to pioneering history-changing projects. In the midst of challenging times—and we are in the thick of them now—channeling our inner Rosalies can change the world.

HER LEGACY

Rosalie Edge marched from a life of privilege to the bristly front lines of conservation warfare, an amateur bird-watcher who wouldn't stand for continued sacrilege of wildlife. She wasn't steeped in experience or bathed in prestigious education; she simply cared and did something about it—a lot of something. Edge defined grassroots activism in her day, mired in the Great Depression, and became the conservation movement's First Lady for three decades.

She followed Hawk Mountain with highly visible nationwide crusades leading to the establishment of Washington's Olympic National Park and Kings Canyon National Park in California's Sierra Nevada. When 8,000 acres of old-growth pines at Yosemite National Park were sentenced to quick death by the saw, Edge lobbied Congress to purchase the land and save the trees, subsequently tightening environmental protection standards there and at Yellowstone. Hers was the loudest voice against pesticide use at the time, and she nearly singlehandedly shaped the nascent years of environmental activism. Some of history's most influential names, including Carson, Sierra Club powerhouse David Brower, Roger Tory Peterson, and many more built their careers from Edge's influence.

Edge never relented on the critical importance—nay, our very duty—to impart personal responsibility for biodiversity and balance in Nature. Among her annals of tireless dedication, Hawk Mountain Sanctuary and the Rosalie Edge Society offer the most visible and enduring gift by protecting birds of prey through targeted research and education: a just and deserved legacy for an indomitable hellcat.

MARJORY STONEMAN DOUGLAS

1890–1998

COURTESY THE STATE LIBRARY AND ARCHIVES OF FLORIDA

The Everglades is a test. If we pass it, we may get to keep the planet.

"Lay aside your cloak, O Birch-tree!
Lay aside your white-skin wrapper,
For the Summer-time is coming,
And the sun is warm in heaven,
And you need no white-skin wrapper!"
Thus aloud cried Hiawatha

And the tree with all its branches
Rustled in the breeze of morning,
Saying, with a sigh of patience,

"Take my cloak, O Hiawatha!"

MARJORY STONEMAN DOUGLAS CRIED WHEN HER FATHER READ
this passage of Henry Wadsworth Longfellow's *Song of Hiawatha*.
More than a reaction to a sad story, the ode mirrored a young girl's
attraction to Nature that would influence her own writing and
place her as one of the 20th century's preeminent conservation
influencers. But, first, there were orange trees.

On a trip to Havana with her parents, a four-year-old Marjory frolicked among orange trees at a layover stop in Florida,
something the native Minnesotan certainly wasn't used to. The
tropical getaway changed her life. "I never forgot the quality of
the tropic light as if I had been looking for it all the years of gray
northern light; as I came back many years later, I recognized it as
something I had loved and missed and longed for all my life, one
of the things that made me so happy about being in Florida."

Two years after her first glimpse of oranges attached to trees,
and wide-open oceans, Marjory's parents separated and her
mother toted them off to Massachusetts. The tenuous extended
family environment nudged Marjory deeper into reading, a place
of solace and inspiration, and soon she was writing, as well, contributing stories at age 16 to *St. Nicholas* magazine (the same
publication featuring work from her compatriot Rachel Carson).
She reveled in research and learning, scouring libraries "knowing
that there was so much that I could put my hands on."

"All we need, really, is a change from a near frigid to a tropical
attitude of mind."

That educational delight fueled the start of Marjory's studies at Wellesley College and a time of new personal discovery. She secured an engaging circle of friends and an enduring connection to Nature, spent her senior year as editor of the college annual, and continued writing award-winning work leading up to graduation (with straight As from start to finish) with a bachelor's degree in English in 1912.

Celebration and plans to start an exhilarating career were short-lived, however, when her mother, Lillian, began losing her battle with cancer. Marjory quickly returned home but Lillian died later that year. Marjory circled in and out of several jobs and wound up marrying an older man who appeared the consummate gentleman but turned out to be a con artist snake intending to swindle her father, Frank, who recognized trouble and urged Marjory (now Douglas) to end the marriage and join him in Miami.

> "Don't think it is enough to attend meetings and sit there like a lump. . . . It is better to address envelopes than to attend foolish meetings. It is better to study than act too quickly; but it is best to be ready to act intelligently when the appropriate opportunity arises. . . . Be a nuisance where it counts, but don't be a bore at any time."

At age 25, Douglas stepped off a train on Florida's sunny Atlantic coast when Miami's population barely reached 5,000. She vividly remembered her first trip there so long ago. This one would be permanent, and life changing, starting with her first job. At the time, her father was publisher of the *News Record*, Miami's first daily newspaper (later becoming the *Miami Herald*) and Douglas joined the staff as a society columnist while Frank engaged in an editorial battle with Florida's governor, Napoleon Bonaparte Broward. Broward's blood coursed with a lust to fill Florida with agriculture and development, and he made numerous bids to drain the Everglades in that regard, essentially trumpeting a call to hordes of so-called community developers driving the state's already meteoric growth.

Like frontier wilderness lands across the country, Florida was vulnerable to development spoilage. In the newsroom, Douglas noticed the threat. Writing about tea parties and high society festivities was slow going, and she spiced things up with environmental news or, in one case, a stint in the Navy. On assignment for a story on the first Miami woman to join the US Naval Reserve, the interviewee never showed so Douglas made her own story by enlisting herself. A bold move, to be sure, but Navy life of waking early and performing humdrum administrative chores didn't align with Douglas's style. She requested a discharge and made a roughly parallel move to the Paris duty station of the American Red Cross for war relief efforts.

After the war, Douglas returned to the *Miami Herald* as assistant editor, quickly garnering popularity and a devoted audience for *The Galley*, her new daily column. The column always started with a poem and then took off in random directions—Douglas wrote in support of women's suffrage, sensible urban planning (Miami's population grew by 100,000 in just 10 years), Prohibition, and improved sanitation infrastructure in segregated areas of the city.

> "It is a woman's business to be interested in the environment. It's an extended form of housekeeping."

Nature also commanded increased presence in Douglas's work, in tandem with her appreciation of Florida's rich and dynamic natural resources, their history, and, more importantly, their precarious future. She deftly leveraged the respect she had earned at the *Herald* to show readers Florida's compelling geography, promoted open space, introduced the frontier Everglades

SPECIAL SPECIES

In a similar refrain heard around the world, wildlife in the Everglades struggle with significant habitat loss. The Everglades once stretched uninterrupted from Orlando to Miami; today, less than half remains. This perpetual wetland environment is home to species found nowhere else on Earth. The snail kite, for instance, is one of the world's most specialized raptors, with a curved bill evolved over millennia to pry apple snails from their shells. These birds have been listed as endangered since 1967 and live only in the Everglades.

American crocodiles live in a mix of fresh and saltwater, and coastal estuaries in South Florida are prime, but dwindling, habitat. This is the only place on Earth where crocs and freshwater-living alligators live together, but water diversion threatens the balance.

Florida panthers are our country's last puma subspecies found in the East, nearly extinct due to disappearing and disconnected habitat. Conservation efforts are helping and panther numbers today are estimated at between 120 and 250.

and its quirky residents, and wrote of hurricane challenges and virtually anything else about her adopted home state. She left the paper in 1923 but continued writing prolifically, publishing more than one hundred articles by 1990, forty of which appeared in the *Saturday Evening Post*.

Douglas's world changed again on a 1928 trip to the Everglades to gauge its potential for protection as a national park. Joining her were National Park Service and Audubon Society heavy hitters, a renowned botanist, and a US representative. It took 20 years, but the Everglades was formerly established as a national park in 1947, protecting the country's largest subtropical wilderness, the 1.5-million-acre lungs of Florida. Several years prior to the new park's introduction, an editor approached Douglas with a pitch to write a book on the Miami River, which she accepted, but accompanying research on the Everglades captivated her far more than the river. She redirected the book's main character and was off to the races.

National park status helped, but threats to the Everglades persisted, including the Tamiami Trail highway (today's US 41 slicing right through the Everglades' heart). Douglas had a talent for vibrant writing on Nature and dove into 5 years of research, her favorite pastime. The Everglades have an incredibly rich cultural and ecological history, yet little was known at the time. Douglas complemented her work partnering with Garald Parker, a USGS and Florida state hydrologist who discovered the Everglades is responsible for refilling the Biscayne Aquifer, South Florida's only water source. Douglas likened clear, fresh water flowing from Lake Okeechobee to a river of grass, and her book's title was born. *The Everglades: River of Grass* was published in 1947, selling out its first printing in a month.

Douglas knew the Everglades was an incomparable ecosystem inexorably linked to Florida's populations (human and wild). Sadly, while she wrote her book, the Everglades burned. In a headstrong race to clear the land for farming and development, cattle farmers set alight infernos that roared uncontrolled, planes screamed by dropping fire bombs or unleashed a confetti of smoldering cigarette butts to light more fires, developers drained water as fast as they could, and remaining water seemed to retreat to whatever hidden recesses it could find. Mayhem. Disrespect. Ignorance. Greed.

In *River of Grass*, Douglas wrote of the Everglades' incomparable diversity and tenuous hold on life:

> *They are unique in the simplicity, the diversity, the related harmony of the forms of life that they enclose.*
>
> *There must be progress, certainly. But we must ask ourselves what kind of progress we want, and what price we want to pay for it. If, in the name of progress, we want to destroy*

everything beautiful in our world, and contaminate the air we breathe, and the water we drink, then we are in trouble.

"There are no other Everglades in the world." The first line from Douglas's seminal work, a statement as powerful in truth as brevity, was adopted for the park's website welcome page and reveals a mindset that should prevail in all things Nature. *River of Grass* catapulted Douglas into her "second career" as Grand Dame of the Everglades, and of conservation as a whole, for the next five decades. The book woke people up to the travesty happening right in front of them and united a movement to protect one of Florida's most visible and critical resources, and gave the Everglades its due in attracting droves of tourists. Nearly 75 years after its publication, her book still serves as powerful reference to the Everglades' constant threats of doom.

She never stopped writing and routinely received invitations to speak on conservation issues around the nation. "Whoever wants me to talk, I'll come over and tell them about the necessity of preserving the Everglades." In 1969 she founded Friends of the Everglades to further advance conservation and preservation support, leading the way with a fierce disposition that moved mountains.

I'm an old lady. I've got white hair, I've been around here forever, and no one can afford to be rude to me. And don't think I don't take advantage of that. I say outrageous things and get away with it.

Her most moving parting words, to me, say it all:

Do your part to inform and stimulate the public to join your action. . . . Be depressed, discouraged, and disappointed at failure and the disheartening effects of ignorance, greed, corruption, and bad politics—but never give up.

HER LEGACY

"The miracle of the light pours over the green and brown expanse of saw grass and of water, shining and slow-moving below, the grass and water that is the meaning and the central fact of the Everglades of Florida. It is a river of grass."

Marjory Stoneman Douglas lived 108 years, a great many of those years with ferocious dedication to extraordinary natural spaces. Her impact was enormous, of course, in her beloved Florida but felt as well around the world.

She helped knock down stubborn proposals (like those inflatable clown punching bags that keep standing up after you punch 'em over) to build a giant aviation runway smack in the middle of the Everglades, rejected equally boneheaded ideas to redirect naturally flowing water through expansive sawgrass, and helped in efforts to restore the area's native ecosystem. Today, the Everglades is in the midst of a comprehensive, unprecedented restoration project, similar in scope to reviving the world's coral reefs. It is the most extensive of its kind in history, anywhere on Earth, and Douglas's book remains on shelves of scientists and engineers as a go-to reference manual on how to get it done. In her lifetime alone, she helped save a vast wilderness in the cross-hairs of development and resource exploitation. The Everglades is now a national park, International Biosphere Reserve, Wetland of International Significance, and Cartagena Treaty specially pro-tected area. The park itself boasts North America's largest stand of sawgrass, the Western Hemisphere's largest protected mangrove ecosystem, critical habitat for threatened and endangered spe-cies, and more than one million acres designated as the Marjory Stoneman Douglas Wilderness.

The honors don't stop there. Florida's Department of Envi-ronmental Protection named its Tallahassee headquarters after her, and the National Parks Conservation Association has a Marjory Stoneman Douglas Award honoring "individuals who often must go to great lengths to advocate and fight for the protection of the National Park System." She was posthumously inducted into the National Wildlife Federation Hall of Fame (1999) and the National Women's Hall of Fame (2000), and Queen Elizabeth II traveled to Florida to meet Douglas in 1991. When she turned 100, Douglas asked people to plant trees around Florida. And plant they did—more than 100,000 trees throughout the state. In 1993, President Bill Clinton awarded Douglas the Medal of Freedom, with this dedication:

> *Beyond Florida, Marjory Stoneman Douglas is a mentor for all who desire to preserve what we southerners affectionately call "a sense of place." And, Mrs. Douglas, the next time I hear someone mention the timeless wonders and powers of Mother Nature, I'll be thinking of you.*

Douglas donated her medal to Wellesley College.

Most of all, her life's work inspired millions of people to look for their own wild places, in their backyards or states or countries, go into them, and fight to keep them.

"There is always the need to carry on."

DAVID BROWER
1912–2000

THANKS TO THE COLBY MEMORIAL LIBRARY, SIERRA CLUB,
FOR USE OF ITS HISTORICAL ARCHIVES.

*We don't inherit the earth from our ancestors, we borrow it
from our children.*

*The Archdruid was a fledgling, bright-eyed California boy.
He tinkered with a creek one day and the next held his blind
mother's hand on walks in the woods. As a young man, he
trained soldiers and fought with them in war. When the fighting stopped, he gathered friends to protect a river, built parks,
scaled peaks, and started a movement. Then he went to the top*

of a mountain, his solace, and died. The people below looked up and heard with the wind, "Let us begin. Let us restore the Earth. Let the mountains talk, and the rivers run. Once more, and forever."

IN HIS 1971 CONSERVATION EPIC, *ENCOUNTERS WITH THE ARCHdruid,* seminal author John McPhee relates tales of an environmentalist's confrontations with a trio of enemies. The Archdruid is David Brower, father of the modern environmental movement and one of Earth's most devoted and prolific protectors. From *Encounters:*

"When Brower was a small boy in Berkeley, he used to build dams in Strawberry Creek, on the campus of the University of California, piling up stone in arcs convex to the current, backing up reservoir ponds. Then he would kick the dams apart and watch the floods that returned Strawberry Creek to its free-flowing natural state."

Years later, he stood on a ridge overlooking what used to be Arizona's Glen Canyon, the Cathedral in the Desert, and felt failure. An enormous cement horseshoe dam submerged the Cathedral, a place of isolated grace carved over epochs, beneath a "lake" created by hundreds of feet of the Colorado River's manhandled water. McPhee tells us that Brower believed the dam represented "the greatest failure of his life" and its very existence was his fault, that more awareness and preparation could have prevented the dam's unfathomable destruction, often referred to as "America's most regretted environmental mistake." Most certainly, Brower didn't go down without one hell of a fight.

"To me, a wilderness is where the flow of wildness is essentially uninterrupted by technology; without wilderness the world is a cage."

In early 1900s Berkeley, Brower's outdoors-loving parents toted their young son along on many camping and hiking adventures in the close-at-hand Sierra Nevada Mountains. Brower's father taught mechanical drawing at the University of California's young campus, a then-undeveloped and largely, blissfully wild, playground for a curious, solitary kid.

Tragedy struck early, however, when Brower's mother developed an inoperable brain tumor and lost her sight from complications following his younger brother's birth. But the family leveraged the positive, and Brower quickly assumed a great deal of maturity by design—helping his mother adapt to a new life, guiding her on walks around Berkeley neighborhoods and then farther afield in the nearby hills. She loved walking those hills, especially to the top of Grizzly Peak, the second highest of the Berkeley region. Verbally relating vivid details in "showing" her trees and flowers and wildlife, Brower's own appreciation of wilderness soared.

One day, he slowed his mother to a halt while he watched a butterfly evolving before his eyes on a milkweed plant. It seemed a struggle, and he attempted to help by tearing the seam of the chrysalis but interrupted Nature's flow. The butterfly died. Brower was devastated but the moment imprinted a message of letting things be that would define his life.

Brower attended UC Berkeley at age 16 (his father had since lost his position there), intent on studying entomology, but dropped out after two years, following the siren song of the mountains. The refrain initially got him only as far as a concession stand job at Yosemite, but the park was in the high country, providing easy access to weeks-long, tentless expeditions. By this time, Brower was a strapping lad tough as boot leather with climbing skills burrowed into craggy hands that soon led guests from Echo Lake Camp into Yosemite's wilderness. In the midst of three years guiding visitors on backcountry trips, someone showed

Brower a Sierra Club Bulletin, laying the foundation of a storied, tumultuous, wildly influential career.

Brower was hooked and immediately joined the Sierra Club (his membership sponsored by friend and legendary photographer Ansel Adams), leveraging his Yosemite experience to a trip leader position shepherding groups 200-strong into the High Sierra, the place he felt most at peace. The mountains indeed were part and parcel to Brower's success notching seventy first ascents across the country, including New Mexico's Shiprock, a heretofore stubbornly resistant rock to the climbing faithful. It was this ascent where Brower's team pioneered the early use of expansion bolts.

Throughout his time in rarified alpine air and distant wilderness reaches, Brower's environmental ideals adopted similar accord. In 1935, Yosemite National Park hired him as a publicity manager, and he rapidly became an active and vocal wilderness advocate. The more time he spent out there, the more driven he was to protect it.

"It seems that every time mankind is given a lot of energy, we go out and wreck something with it."

Then things got interesting. In 1941, Brower held an editorial role at the University of California Press and earned a seat on the Sierra Club's Board of Directors. A year later, he edited the *Manual of Ski Mountaineering* used for training World War II mountain troops and capped it off by enlisting as a mountaineering guide, first training 10th Mountain Division troops stateside and joining them soon after in combat in Italy, for which he received a Bronze Star.

Back in the States following the war, Brower edited the Sierra Club Bulletin and settled into the executive director chair in 1952. His leadership during that tenure has been called extreme, militant, and, on a quiet day, controversial, but over a 17-year stretch, club membership saw a tenfold swell from 7,000 to 70,000, transforming the Sierra Club from a laid-back gaggle of hikers to one of the world's most influential conservation organizations, augmenting wilderness protection with policy development driving change in other arenas.

Brash and rarely willing to compromise ideals or direction, Brower rubbed many of his colleagues the wrong way. Nevertheless, he was the ringleader behind many of the club's biggest wins. He leveraged his power of persuasion to funnel enormous publicity streams into the importance of saving the world. And it worked. He launched a Sierra Club publishing division and teamed with Ansel Adams to produce their first product: a hefty coffee table book loaded with stunning nature photography. From there came a succession of similar heavyweight titles in oversize format, calendars, and other publications laden with narrative and images aimed to inspire, reminiscent of Brower's own tenets:

From citizenship comes responsibility to care.

Polite conversationalists leave no mark save the scars upon the Earth that could have been prevented had they stood their ground.

Sierra published more than seventy books throughout Brower's life and ushered in a new era of media advocacy for Nature, striking a call to arms with three generations of fervent youth. Seemingly overnight, swarms of people pulsing with wanderlust blood slung backpacks over their shoulders and beelined to the Sierra Nevada to celebrate and revel in wilderness. Trumpeting loudest in written form was Terry and Renny Russell's *On the Loose*, a story of two brothers' reverence and discovery of Nature traveling around the West. The conservation movement was on, infused with 1960s free thinking and an influx of newly protected wild lands. Consider Point Reyes, California, on the real estate chopping block and doomed to become a San Francisco suburb. Brower led a fierce battle against a sea of future rooftops and, in 1962, President Kennedy signed a bill establishing Point Reyes National Seashore, protecting some of the nation's most sacred coastline.

> "The more we pour the big machines, the fuel, the pesticides, the herbicides, the fertilizer and chemicals into farming, the more we knock out the mechanism that made it all work in the first place."

Brower visited Point Reyes often, relishing the spirit of the place, the surf, the serrated cliffs. His wife, Ann, remarked on the gleam in her husband's eyes, "He's just fun to be with outdoors. The smallest little thing, he found fascinating. You'd think about things newly, the way you would with a small child." Indeed, Brower had a humble view of Nature; he wanted "to just experience the wildness that the ages have made perfect; it's the thing I like."

And he wouldn't allow anything to get in the way. In staunch opposition to the Glen Canyon Dam, he ran a full-page ad in the *New York Times*, denouncing the project with a pointed question to readers: "Should we also flood the Sistine Chapel so tourists can get nearer the ceiling?" The ad galvanized the nation's attention on the ruinous scheme but also rankled many Sierra Club execs; he was fired two years later.

Brower wasn't fazed. In his crusade to save the world, he simply reset and founded Friends of the Earth, a powerhouse global environmental network still active in more than fifty countries, and co-founded its sister organization, League of Conservation Voters, America's most visible and instrumental environment-focused political action group, now with satellite locations around the world. Brower also established Earth Island Institute supporting global activist projects, as well as the John Muir Institute for Environmental Studies, North Cascades Conservation Council, Fate of the Earth Conferences, and many others.

INSPIRING LEADERS

Earth Island Institute's New Leaders Initiative (NLI) program hosts the annual Brower Youth Award honoring its founder and young, eager successors to his environmental mission. NLI helps foster greater capacity and accessibility for the newest generation of environmental activists. Recent award winners work in areas including plastic pollution, organic produce, Indigenous climate change education, and industrial pollution.

Among his climactic touch points was overpopulation, appallingly absent from current environmental conversations. Brower long ago saw the impending doom of an overcrowded planet and infused the issue into much of his work, albeit to consistent pushback if not outright ignorance. The Sierra Club itself, for example, discounted overpopulation and immigration as serious problems, fueling Brower's resignation, yet he continued pushing for increased understanding with controversial (prophetic?) statements. "Childbearing should be a punishable crime against society, unless the parents hold a government license."

You don't have a conservation policy unless you have a population policy.

Population is pollution spelled inside out.

His career was equal parts radical, pioneer, and savior, described thusly: "The Sierra Club made the Nature Conservancy look reasonable. I founded Friends of the Earth to make the Sierra Club look reasonable. Then I founded Earth Island Institute to make Friends of the Earth look reasonable. Earth First! now makes us look reasonable. We're still waiting for someone else to come along and make Earth First! look reasonable."

Powering Brower's conservation engine room was his desire to ignite a sense of place in the younger generation, engaging in personal, productive conversations to learn what drives them and how best to harness that energy toward a just and balanced Earth—a solid strategy to confront and manage the procession of environmental crises facing us today.

We could use a cavalry of people like Brower in our new world normal of climate change and related catastrophes in everyday news. His entire being functioned with Nature's heartbeat and an obstinate-yet-moving maternal responsibility to action and purpose that, for better or worse, overwhelmed traditional life accoutrements, including friends and family.

Maligned in the media and the environmental movement for so-called militant and damned stubborn ways, many people believe Brower's rough-around-the-edges reputation was fostered by the media and corporate entities themselves. A fellow environmentalist on Brower's influence: "Calling David Brower an important environmental activist is like calling Hamlet an important member of the Danish royal court. Brower invented modern American environmental activism."

David Brower was a fierce environmental activist—the only way activists can accomplish anything—caring less about his reputation than the far more pressing goal of protecting Nature's special places. He dedicated his life to the cause and for that we can all be grateful.

"This island of Earth of ours is finite in resources, including wilderness—particularly wilderness. The dwindling worldwide reservoir of wild lands must be the concern of everyone, but especially of those of us who have been privileged to experience wildness, and thus learn its value to the individual human soul and to the spirit of mankind."

HIS LEGACY

"We must begin thinking like a river if we are to leave a legacy of beauty and life for future generations."

David Brower was born two years prior to the death of John Muir, widely recognized as history's most influential conservationist, to whom he is often compared. With zeal equal to his successor, Brower carried on Muir's legacy, dedicating 70 years of ardent activism to protect America's wilderness.

He dove into the environmental movement's earliest days and defined it with a succession of monumental victories—halting Bureau of Land Management dam projects in their tracks at Grand Canyon and Dinosaur National Monument, spearheading lobbies establishing an array of celebrity national parks from Cape Cod to Redwood to Point Reyes, and leveraging his Sierra Club years to drive creation of the Wilderness Act. He was a writer, publisher, filmmaker, activist, speaker, teacher, and leader nominated three times for the Nobel Peace Prize and received 1998's Blue Planet Prize for his significant dedication to Nature's most pressing issues. The American Alpine Club's David R. Brower Award recognizes "leadership and commitment to conservation and the preservation of mountain regions worldwide."

In the publishing arena, book reviewer Mal Warwick sums up Brower's influence with a stroke of potent brevity: "David Brower was a genius. He was a seminal figure in the history of humankind's effort to right our balance with Nature."

Will we ever attain that balance? Set aside our penchant for dominating for penance of same? Possibly, but the balance must be tipped in Nature's favor to regain composure.

"If I could go back to a point in history to try to get things to come out differently, I would go back and tell Moses to go up the mountain again and get the other tablet. Because the Ten Commandments just tell us what we are supped to do with one another, not a word about our relationship to the earth. Genesis starts with these commands: multiply, replenish the earth, and subdue it. We have multiplied very well, we have replenished our populations very well, we have subdued it all too well, and we don't have any other instruction."

"The wild places are where we began. When they end, so do we."

JOHN FRANCIS

1946–

COURTESY JOHN FRANCIS

Silence is always with us. But we do not choose silence, silence chooses us. If you are called to be silent on your journey, recognize the invitation as a great gift. It is a gift to be shared with others. Your relationship to silence is one thing that will define the uniqueness of your journey.

IF A GIANT OIL TANKER CARRYING 106,000 GALLONS OF BUNKER fuel leaves San Francisco Bay at 1 a.m. motoring at 15 knots in dense fog and zero visibility, and another tanker leaves the same bay loaded with 115,000 barrels of crude oil, also traveling at 15 knots, how long will it be until they crash?

The answer is 1:45 a.m. in a horrifying math problem come to life. Both Standard Oil tankers, the *Arizona Standard* and *Oregon Standard*, were going too fast for conditions, no doubt confident in their state-of-the-art radar and foghorns to predict and warn away trouble. But neither ship captain nor crew were completely sure if they were in the center of the channel and didn't stick to the star-board side, what you're supposed to do when driving an enormous ship in the dark. Later reports also confirmed the crews were not properly operating their radars.

The next sound they heard was a guttural, sickening tear of metal as the *Arizona* embedded its bow 40 feet into the *Oregon*, through which poured more than 800,000 gallons of putrid, chemical-laced crude. US Coast Guard and Standard Oil ships leaped into action, trying to suck up the oil with vacuum hoses and collection booms. It didn't work. Within 12 hours the oozing slick reached Fisherman's Wharf, the Marin County coastline, and Berkeley Marina. Much of the oil rode tides and contaminated beaches 40 miles south and 20 miles north of the bay.

John Francis was in San Francisco that January 1971 day as the event unfolded, the largest and most devastating oil spill in Bay Area history. (It's disturbing that oil spills happen so often they have a history and different levels of awfulness. All spills are devastating.) Francis had come to California from his native Philadelphia, lured west like so many others. Not long before, he worked the land with his aunt and uncle on their Virginia farm, sowing and harvesting food and nurturing a country-borne work ethic. A near-constant pull to travel pried him away, and he brought a deep love of the outdoors and insatiable attraction to geography to Marin County. Francis never shied from hefting on a backpack and wandering, and similar to legions of like-minded souls of the day, tuned further into environmental perils after reading *Silent Spring*.

On that January day, he witnessed peril in real time. Sensitive wildlife habitats and native coastline were in the crosshairs of ink-black death. Frightened and confused bird species—western grebes, scoters, ducks, and many more—fled to shore, where frightened and confused residents tried to help them but no one knew what to do. Nevertheless, thousands of area residents and visitors marched to the shore to rescue stranded or dying wildlife and clean up beaches. The united forces directly influenced the early days of pollution activism and a number of environmental groups sprang from the ooze.

By March, state officials estimated (conservatively) 7,000 birds covered in oily filth. Most of them died on shore or stuck in the water-borne slick before rescuers could reach them. The spill decimated the area's avian species. Volunteers rescued more than 4,000 birds but then what? How do you care for waterfowl saturated in oil? The outcome was bleak; only around 300 birds gained enough strength to return to the wild. One silver lining was the volunteer upswell contributed to International Bird Rescue, a brand-new organization based in aquatic bird rehabilitation and research.

John Francis was on the beach in the thick of cleanup, shocked and outraged, scrubbing oil and helping save the lives of defenseless sea life. It felt good to join hundreds of his brethren in the efforts, but the fragility of life hit home and something stirred inside; after this was over, he wanted to contribute to Earth's protection in his own way. Looking around at clogged city traffic, Francis decided to hang up his car keys and walk. Wherever he needed to go, he would get there on foot: no cars, buses, trains, planes—anything with a motor was off limits.

"As my father stretches to understand my journey, I realize that maybe you can't change the world by your actions alone, but you can change yourself. And when you do, the world around you may change by attempting to understand you, as we all try to understand each other."

Family reacted in surprise, friends didn't believe he could do it, people on the street mocked him. But he kept walking, fueled with a self-described sense of arrogance fully expecting his message to attract the masses to join him. "My highest goal was to walk around the planet in the hope that I could benefit mankind. I didn't know what I meant to be a benefit, but I hoped along the way, with my education, I could somehow make the planet a better place."

On his birthday in 1973, still restless from the oil spill spectacle, Francis was intrigued with the idea of not talking and, instead, really listening to others—not simply their words but what meaning they held. What did they have to say? What stories, life events, or true-to-heart feelings did they have to share? The experience fascinated him, and he remained silent the next day as well, and the one after that. "For the first time, I began to listen and what I heard kind of disturbed me." His one-day whim took hold and became a *17-year* vow of silence. With the exception of a single phone call to his mother after a decade of silence, Francis didn't utter a word.

From this new place lessons come, or perhaps realizations. The first is that most of my adult life I have not been listening fully. I only listened long enough to determine whether the speaker's ideas matched my own. If they did not, I would stop listening and my mind would race ahead to compose an argument against what I believed the speaker's idea or position to be, which I would interject at the first opportunity. Giving myself permission not to speak, not to attack some idea or position, also gives me permission to listen fully. Giving myself this permission gives the speaker permission to speak fully their idea or position without fear of rebuttal in a way that I could not have imagined.

In a place of inner peace and purpose, he combined his silence and walking and set off with a backpack and a banjo, looking every part the free-spirit vagabond. He walked everywhere, no

EARTH DAY AND OIL WELLS

The origins of Earth Day ironically date back to an oil spill just 2 years prior to the San Francisco tanker collision. A Union Oil platform off the Santa Barbara coast blew out, unleashing more than three million gallons of oil into the sea, killing untold thousands of seabirds, dolphins, fish, and other ocean life. Activists banded together to fight for environmental regulation, culminating with Wisconsin senator Gaylord Nelson's push to establish nationwide environmental awareness. Held each April, Earth Day continues to educate, celebrate, and drive change.

matter how far—the width of the United States (twice), the length of South America with a side trip to Antarctica, Australia's Great Ocean Road, and a veritable dot-to-dot walk between US colleges he attended.

He has been known as Planetwalker ever since. When he needed to communicate with others, he used gestures, writing, and even his banjo. (Banjo strings are full of great stories.) Aside from spreading an environmental awareness message with every step, what did Francis do with himself out there?

He earned a PhD, of course. Far from the traditional path to higher education, he first walked up to Southern Oregon State University in Ashland and completed a two-year bachelor's degree. Eager to continue the momentum, he got in touch with the University of Montana–Missoula to reserve a space in their Environmental Studies master's program, two years hence. Why the delay? He had to get there first, starting with a walk north to Washington to build a boat, commencing a long sailing-walking journey to his first day of class.

With diploma in hand (tucked into his backpack), he thought he might as well keep going and walked east to the University of Wisconsin–Madison to commence doctoral studies on—what else?—the effects of oil spills. Keep in mind that all this happened while Francis remained utterly silent. Like most doctoral students, Francis taught a class (Resources Management), but did so using only sign language, writing on a board, and even miming. He soon earned a PhD in Land Resources from UW's Gaylord Nelson Institute, about the same time as the Exxon Valdez fiasco, and walked to Washington, DC, to his new project manager job with the US Coast Guard's Oil Pollution Act, contributing to writing oil spill regulations. He ended his 17-year vow of silence on Earth Day, 1990. Speaking to a crowd pulsing with anticipation to hear his first words, Francis said, "Thank you for being here. After 17 years of not speaking, I know the importance of there being someone there to hear what you have to say." In an unfortunate twist, he was hit by a car the next day. In true Francis fashion, however, he begged off the ambulance and walked to the hospital for treatment.

By 1994, Francis realized he could boost his impact by using the more rapid transit of vehicles to reach more locations and people in communicating what he saw as a direct correlation between societal and environmental problems. "We are all really part of the environment. How we treat each other is how we treat the environment." He strongly believes that an overwhelming lack of empathy and connection among people has us mired in our current environmental emergencies.

And what thoughts on his walking pilgrimage, part inner reflection, part wanderlust, part communique? "The commitment to walking requires tremendous tenacity. Each day you discover who you are and being that person is challenging and exciting." He is no less enamored with travel and the great big world's tangible and cerebral rewards. "Geography is something that affects us, and we affect it; it is both an inner and outer experience. The outer experience is tangible—we can physically see and interact with the environment. The inner portion, however, is a journey that some of us go on, and one that we may go on without actually traveling very far. It is a journey of self-discovery."

"As you walk look around, assess where you are, reflect on where you have been, and dream of where you are going. Every moment of the present contains the seeds of opportunity for change."

In another Earth Day monument, Francis retraced his original walk across America, intent on reshaping today's environmental issues as inclusive to everyone. He looked closely for changes in the physical landscape as well as conversations that could inspire partnerships with all cultures, corporations, and organizations with long track records of not seeing eye to eye on the environment. He remains stalwart today in a belief that humans are part (not lords) of Nature and our behavior has a tremendous impact on the place we depend on.

To that end, Francis founded Planetwalk, a nonprofit with a mission to develop a global network of Planetwalkers by sponsoring organized walks in the United States and globally to promote environmental education and foster a more peaceful, cooperative world. Today, Francis regularly speaks to audiences worldwide in support of the environment's role in the travel industry, ethics in humanitarian efforts, and diversity among the world's conservation organizations.

Most of all he urges students, young people, all of us to *listen*.

"If we treat each other better, naturally, we treat the world better."

HIS LEGACY

"Your life is an adventure. Live it fully."

It is only appropriate that John Francis contributed to rewriting oil transportation regulations and spill mitigation guidelines. He took his work a step higher by channeling efforts to increase environmental education and awareness on a global scale. Part of his focus derives from Planetlines, the feature attraction of Planetwalk, that he describes as an innovative, modular curriculum for grades K-12 and beyond to college students and use by the general public. The program encourages direct interaction with our environment through walking, where the outdoors becomes the classroom and students learn through contact with the world around them.

> "I watch the blue jays, 50 or more, that come down each day swooping easily from limb to limb with raucous laughter, feet curled under. And in the quiet I hear the voice of the river passing among the rocks and over stones, everywhere at once, making its way through steep green canyons to the sea. I try to catch the words mingling with the shushing of the trees. Perhaps this is where our speech began. Maybe long ago before there were words, there was only the river and the people listened to the water. . . and the quiet whispering."

Francis still walks for noble causes, such as throughout Cuba studying the country's organic agriculture and application of sustainable development. In 2010, he became the National Geographic Society's first Education Fellow, and was also appointed the United Nations Environment Program's Goodwill Ambassador to the World's Grassroots Communities.

> "A lot of times we find ourselves in this wonderful place where we've gotten to, but there is another place for us to go and we kind of have to leave behind the security of who we've become and go to the place we are becoming."

MARTIN LITTON

1917–2014

ARA MARDEROSIAN, SEQUOIA FORESTKEEPER

"Be reasonable!" they say. But I never felt it did any good to be reasonable about anything in conservation, because what you give away will never come back—ever.

AN OCTOBER 1935 EDITION OF THE *LOS ANGELES TIMES* PRINTED a letter from then-18-year-old Martin Litton who wrote in part, "The people of the entire state should rise up against the destruction of Mono Lake. Mono Lake is a gem—among California's greatest scenic attractions—a beautiful and historic landmark which must not be destroyed."

At age 89, after 70 years of vehement environmental activism, Litton became the oldest person to run the Colorado River, America's third longest, through the Grand Canyon. It seemed only yesterday when people wanted to celebrate him running the river at 80, but Litton shrugged it off. "Eighty, hell. The significance is trivial. People say you're the oldest guy to row the canyon. Well, I've been that for 20 years. How many 60-year-olds do you see doing this?" Today, many thousands run the canyon's frothy rapids, and few are six decades in.

From the first time he pushed off in 1955, Litton and the Colorado were inseparable. Litton was the 185th person to make the trip (from Lees Ferry to Grand Wash Cliffs) since explorer John Wesley Powell. His thoughts on his milestone river day echoed those from the *Times* letter nearly 70 years earlier: "It's my world and I don't want any other. What it hasn't got is not worth having, and what it doesn't know is not worth knowing." Three years later, in 2004, he made his last river trip at the oars of his beloved dory, wrapping up a storied history. "The Grand Canyon is America's greatest scenic treasure—an experience made to order in wonder," Litton declared. "Floating a boat down the Colorado? Why it's simply the best thing one can do."

Litton's adoration for the outdoors took hold in a class at Inglewood High. He read a book about climbing attempts on Mount Everest and wanted a taste of it, in whatever his local California topography would allow. He fired up the family car (a 1927 Essex!), motored to nearby Mount Baldy, and post-holed through knee-deep snow to the summit. Elated with peak-bagging, he later summited Mount Whitney with a friend and a pack burro rented for 75 cents a day. However, Litton's calling was canyon country, inspired by another high school assignment, this time transcribing portions of Powell's Colorado River expedition journals. The river, the canyons, mystery, adventure—Litton was entranced.

But for the time being, Southern California's canyons had to suffice. Litton went on to attend UCLA, where he started

A FLOATING LEGACY

In classic Martin Litton fashion, he started a tradition of naming the Grand Canyon dories after natural wonders that had been destroyed by man, "to remind us of places we've destroyed without any necessity, so that maybe we'll think twice before we do it again." The tradition expanded to include places not yet vanquished but that certainly deserved fighting for, and in 2015, the OARS group named their newest handcrafted dory *Marble Canyon* in Litton's honor.

California Trails, a club for eager conservationists that served as a launch pad for dozens of articles turned feature news stories. His fiery writing called attention to everything from a Yampa River dam to unchecked logging and piles of highway litter. He left college with an English degree and soon joined the US Army Air Corps, training for and flying missions over Europe in World War II. One mission for the 82nd Airborne's Glider Infantry Wing took a frightening turn when Litton was shot down, spending the next few days hiding in woods and swamps, exchanging gunfire with German soldiers. Fortunately, he made it back safely to Belgium.

Returning to the United States after the war, Litton worked for the *Los Angeles Times* writing about environmental issues and successes. In the early 1950s he felt the exhilaration of rapids on rivers at Dinosaur National Monument in northwestern Colorado and quickly learned of the impending threat of dams. He was furious and joined David Brower (who Litton hailed as the greatest conservationist of all time) and a host of others in blocking the dams' approval, then went on to help protect other rivers, nurturing a decades-long love affair with the Colorado in particular.

With his commanding, baritone voice and surly disposition (he has been known as righteous, cantankerous, grumpy, and a tad irritating), Litton established a growing reputation as a fighter with an ironclad refusal to give in. The modern environmental movement was slowly gaining steam, and his place in the wheelhouse drove it forward. He simply would not stop in defense of Nature and was among the first of his generation to say no to shortsighted, greedy reclamation projects and other environmental travesties. The Grand Canyon itself was targeted for a series of hideous cement impediments, and Litton is widely hailed for stopping the madness.

Even so, the Colorado today is plugged with fifteen major dams along its main course and hundreds (hundreds!) of "lesser" blockades on tributaries. Thanks to the US government's bedding with regional water agencies and corporations that don't give a shit about tomorrow, the Colorado River is one of the world's most heavily developed. In the eye blink span of one century, the river has been mired in a witch's brew of greed, polemic, despair, politics, sickness, and dread. Its waters are siphoned by so many, the river hasn't reached the Gulf of Mexico for decades. A brief spittle now and again in recent years hardly suffices; we have essentially killed off another monument.

Litton didn't take kindly to that kind of behavior, yet his own carried its share of contradictions. He nearly foamed at the mouth in fights to preserve Nature's special places but despised governments' arrogance in telling us where we are "allowed" to go. He preached the gospel of responsible use of our lands but sometimes dumped bags of empty glass bottles into the river after a raft trip. Do we admonish him or offer a pinch of leeway, considering what he accomplished?

On the downside, he joined Brower, Abbey, and so many other conservationists in a crippling defeat. They all battled with a formidable foe (the federal government) to preserve Glen Canyon, a 200-mile-long jewel slated as the highlight feature for Escalante National Park (today's Grand Staircase–Escalante National Monument). This was some of America's most remote land and the last to be formally mapped; today it is entombed in a manufactured embryo hundreds of feet deep called Lake Powell. This reservoir (it doesn't deserve to be called a lake)—essentially a speedboat drag strip, RV magnet, and giant splotch visible from space—boasts a shoreline longer than the entire West Coast. That makes me nauseous.

> "I wish I had accomplished some things in conservation that I did not. We could've stopped Glen Canyon Dam and we didn't, but we didn't try hard enough. We tried very hard in Grand Canyon dams and even harder in Dinosaur National Monument dams—those were our first big issue, and we beat them. Those were said to be necessary for the development of the West. Well we didn't get them built, we fought against them, and they turned out to be unnecessary."

In a grand reversal of fortune, recent conversations have raised the idea of draining the lake to revive Nature. Without the giant Glen Canyon plug, the land can get back to normal. Annual spring floods and dry fall seasons, for example, will go to work rebuilding the canyon's narrow beaches and line canyon walls with vibrant, tenacious flora. With Powell's cold water out of the way, the river's naturally warmer temperatures will help recover native fish and other threatened critters. Drain the lake. Litton, Abbey, and Brower—a trinity of conservation greats—will raise a glass and dance in the heavens.

What about the rest of us, still here with the blessed opportunity to float a river, climb a mountain, walk in the woods, or stand up to save them? How do you describe and feel about *your* favorite places? Litton adored the Colorado River and explained it as such: "I traveled a lot. But no matter what else I saw, this remains the greatest experience on Earth. Are there deeper canyons? Yes. Tougher rivers? Yes. But none of them can compare to what you have here: a river that is almost, but not quite, at the limits of navigation. It's full of exhilaration—the prospect of one exciting moment after another. And the realization of contact with the beauty of the Earth. It's all here. It's a major order of experience."

The gunwales of a boat is the best way to savor that experience. Since Powell and friends first broke trail, rafting the Colorado is a generations-long tradition, first taking firm root in the late 1940s with guided tours in oversize inflatable rafts—"baloney boats"—propelled by motor and canyon-hardened captain. Litton upended tradition and brought the Northeast to the Grand Canyon, preferring sea-tested wooden dories to puffy inflatables ("Voluptuous, pneumatic crafts," Abbey called them). New England–bred and seasoned in the Atlantic's tumultuous waters, as well as the rough and tumble Pacific Northwest, dories are most often wood-and-fiberglass constructed, shallow-draft vessels about 16 feet long, with a flat bottom and high, flared sides. An oarsman sits center, with passengers and gear fore and aft. Litton saw promise for the double-ended river dory popular in Oregon and Washington and adapted the model to the Colorado's surly waters. He started Grand Canyon Dories in 1971, introducing an exhilarating era of river running for two decades that redefined the commercial rafting scene before turning over company reins to the next generation.

All the while, Litton maintained close relationships with Abbey and Brower, among other conservation influencers, in some of history's most important environmental crusades. Without him, we would likely see at least one huge dam in the Grand Canyon, an achievement on its own worthy of a lifetime's merit. But his environmental reach touched areas beyond the canyon walls, as well. Litton served on the Sierra Club's board and the American Land Conservancy and, in a departure from river protection, founded Sequoia ForestKeeper in 2001, the "eyes, ears, and voice of the forest."

He loved the trees like the river and, during his travel editor tenure for *Sunset* magazine, wrote a cover story on California's redwoods, igniting a national conservation campaign and subsequent creation of Redwood National Park. Litton also fought for North Cascades National Park, Idaho's Hells Canyon, and Central California's Diablo Canyon, the latter a Glen Canyon–esque defeat that, at times, pit him against his own people at the Sierra Club. "The Sierra Club gave it away. It was our last chance for a national park on the Central Coast. We had to fight not just developers but our own club. People said we should be reasonable, not extreme. Bull. You can't be constructive. You can't be reasonable. You can't be too extreme. In a compromise, both sides lose. I wasn't against that plant because it was nuclear; I was against building anything there."

> "When it comes to saving wilderness, we can't be extreme enough. To compromise is to lose. When you're willing to compromise your principles you've given up. You abandon them. When you compromise nature, nature gets compromised. It's gone. It's hurt. It's injured. You gain nothing back, ever."

Close friend David Brower saw Litton as his conscience. Sierra Club senior representative Barbara Boyle called him passionate, tempestuous, charming, inappropriate, and impossibly effective.

And talented with a pair of oars, as well. You can watch Litton in action in the riveting National Geographic movie *Martin's Boat*, produced in tandem with OARS, one of the world's foremost adventure companies with deep conservation roots and successor to Litton's Grand Canyon Dories.

America can thank Litton for dozens of environmental success stories, leading the pack with nearly 300 Colorado River miles that still run natural and free, as designed, and it's up to us to ensure it stays that way.

HIS LEGACY

"It doesn't take many voices to make things right, just strong voices."

He was the grand old man of the Colorado River and one of the 20th century's most passionate and influential conservationists. For more than 80 years, Martin Litton worked to protect Nature from mankind's hammer blows and foster a conservation mindset throughout the country. He rallied with the earliest generation of crusaders pushing to expand millions of acres of wilderness areas (or establish new), worked with the National Geographic Society in the creation of Redwood National Park, sparing the big trees from the saw, as well as influencing President Clinton's decision to create Giant Sequoia National Monument.

He was restless to the end of his 97 years, and with good reason. Government and greed are almost always a sure bet for environmental strikes. The Giant Sequoia "protection" lasted about four years before the Forest Service went right back to large-scale logging. Dams remain a constant threat (although that trend is thankfully losing steam). And untold thousands of acres of land are dug up and paved over every year.

Litton's son, John, tells us his dad just wanted it all to stop. "His goal, ever since he was a kid, was to save things that he saw being destroyed. He thought that too many people wanted to destroy things for a buck, and he was trying to say 'stop.' It was to remind everybody where their soul is."

Asked which river trip stands out, Litton described making it through right side up: "Maybe the second one which was the first

time I rowed the boat all the way through with [wife] Esther. . . .
We have to be able to handle all the rapids in the Grand Canyon,
nothing from the shore; everything happens on the river. The boat
makes it through and you hope you'll be right side up at the other
end, and we usually are."

Right side up, on the right side of Nature, his legacy is one
of reverence for wild places and their protection. America thanks
you, Martin.

"What is wilderness? It's mankind's acknowledgment that there
is a higher value, a higher purpose. It ceases to be wilderness
when we're here. But we are its stewards. It is vital to our souls."

CHICO MENDES

1944–1988

ANTONIO SCORZA/STAFF/AFP/©GETTY IMAGES

At first, I thought I was fighting to save rubber trees, then I thought I was fighting to save the Amazon rainforest. Now I realize I am fighting for humanity.

IN 1988, CHICO MENDES TOLD FRIENDS AND FAMILY HE wouldn't live past Christmas. For years, Mendes had fought with verve to curb destruction of his home country's rainforests. Not all of his fellow countrymen felt the same. A few months later, in early December, a shotgun blast slammed into his chest as he walked out the back door of his modest home in Xapuri, Brazil, to wash up for dinner.

At the trigger was Darci Alves da Silva, son of Darli da Silva, a local cattle rancher none too pleased with Mendes's unrelenting campaigns. The ill-tempered family prioritized sprawling cow pastures over saving trees and, to them, Mendes was a liability. Darli allegedly arranged the hit. The father-son team then went on the run but were soon apprehended and tossed in the slammer in December of 1990.

Mendes's murder unleashed international fury and protests, and the US-based Environmental Defense Fund delivered more than 4,000 member letters directly to then-president Fernando Cardoso. A little over two years later, Mendes's killers escaped with a small gang of neighboring prisoners. They simply sawed through the bars of their cells and took off, which was hardly a surprise; the jail wasn't exactly Alcatraz. In fact, the acting secretary of state government at the time commented, "Their escape was expected. If a prisoner does not escape from here, it is because he does not want to." A comprehensive investigation of the escape ensued and the da Silvas were eventually recaptured but still received early release.

Chico Mendes was born in Seringal Santa Fe, a humble village near Xapuri, deep in the Amazon jungle a couple of thousand miles west of Rio de Janeiro's glitz and improvidence. Chico's family was steeped in traditions of rubber trappers and generations-proud harvesting practices for fruits and nuts native to the rainforest. His father, grandfather, and great-grandfather made their living tapping the latex (sap) of rubber trees and selling to commercial buyers.

Mendes joined the family custom at age eight, leaving home ahead of sunrise every day with his father and walking 10 miles of rugged trail, stopping regularly to incise the bark of rubber trees and attach cups to collect slowly draining sap. While the sap oozed out, they hunted for food to bring home—armadillo, peccary, tapir, and monkey. On good days, they returned home with an impressive haul of sap and something for the dinner table.

FADING TREASURES

It's no secret that rainforests are home to thousands of unique plant and animal species, with many more as yet undiscovered—if their habitats withstand human intrusion. Here are the Amazon's top five rarest resident critters.

- Golden lion tamarin monkey—A 1-pound monkey with a lion-like mane. Only about 800 remain.
- Poison dart frog—Colorfully attractive, these diminutive amphibians pack a deadly punch.
- Jaguar—Famously elusive, the beautiful jaguar has the strongest bite of all big cats.
- Amazon manatee—It's a rare treat to spot these gentle giants moving about in their murky water homes.
- River dolphin—This typically shy relative of ocean dolphins favors flood-prone lowland areas

Daily life was challenging and Mendes didn't learn to read or write until age 20, taught by a local activist and fellow rubber trapper. Basic education in hand, Mendes saw the destruction of his native rainforest steamrolling at a sickening pace. Greed and corruption took the form of chainsaws, fire, and bulldozers attacking the forest without mercy. Mendes would not sit idly by while his rainforest home, including rare plants, all the animals living there, and neighboring peoples, suffered malignant treatment.

And the poor behavior started at the top. Brazil's political and military governments went on a tear for more than two decades, from the mid-1960s to mid-1980s, ratifying salvos of self-serving policies that directly threatened the Amazon and its rubber tapping population. The seductive lure of "economic development" (pockets full of money) hooked the government like young love and almost immediately the Amazon's doors were booted wide open for exploitation, and ensuing obliteration, by investors and headstrong cattle ranchers.

Deforestation of unfathomable scale came next and has not skipped a beat ever since. In 2019, smoke from raging, human-ignited fires sullied the skies clear to Sao Paulo. Why the deliberate starting of fires? It's all about cows. Brazil is the world's largest beef exporter and cows need food and places to eat, sleep, poop, and procreate. Fire clears a lot of land quickly—the world has already lost roughly 20 percent of the Amazon rainforest, an indescribable loss and one with critical consequences. The rainforest sucks up billions of tons of carbon, millions of people depend on resources therein, and one in ten of Earth's plant and animal species are found here. The Brazilian government even turned down a substantial foreign aid package to help fight the (deliberately set) fires burning today.

Fire clears Amazon land of people, as well. For decades, Indigenous peoples have been driven from their homelands in the maw of roaring, acrid infernos raging forth like itinerant pits of hell. What defense do they have when faced with 200-foot walls of flame? In just a single decade, 24,000 square miles of rainforest have been wiped clean, the equivalent of more than eight million football fields. Since 1990, more than 500,000 square miles have been lost. Five hundred thousand.

At what cost? Consider the number of rubber trees in that formerly vibrant forest, trees that supported the livelihoods of people harvesting a commodity used by all of us every day. Chico Mendes knew his was but one family of thousands irrevocably affected by rainforest destruction, but he couldn't save the day alone. He needed help and, in 1975, set about forming the Rural Workers' Union and Xapuri Rubber Trappers Union, serving as president of the latter. By the mid-1980s, Mendes had a reputation as a radical activist and fierce union leader with a loyal following. He helped create Brazil's National Council of Rubber Trappers and later established an enduring friendship with the Krenaki people living deep in the rainforest. Together, they formed the Forest People's Movement to mount a more stalwart defense against deforestation.

Money talks, however, and despite proven, long-term profit margins from sustainably harvested, native products such as fruits, nuts, rubber, and an array of medicinal goods, Brazil's government caved under pressure from commercial cattle interests and deforestation only increased. At one point in the 1980s, a raucous group of ranchers drove 100,000 rubber trappers from the forest, sparking Mendes to fight back by gathering workers and their families in forming *empates*, human barricades blocking bulldozers and other implements of destruction.

It worked on enough occasions to alert global environmental groups, and Mendes was soon recognized as the voice of the Amazon. He traveled around the world relating a message of harmonious living with the rainforest, including responsible harvesting and traditional familial practices. Things were all fine and good until that day in 1988 when Darli da Silva wanted to clear-cut a chunk of forest slated for a Nature preserve. Mendes blocked the logging, allowing the creation of the preserve (today's Chico Mendes Ecological Park).

Mendes dedicated his entire life to fighting for the rainforest and was killed for his efforts. His influence remains prevalent, but even his namesake extractive reserve has lost nearly 8 percent of its forest. Clear-cutting throughout Brazil continues unabated, fueling climate change, compromising the rainforest's unique and critical biodiversity, and raising the hackles of those determined to exploit the land for temporary monetary gain. To that end, violence remains an unfortunate byproduct, pitting activists against development, the former of which almost always lose—roughly 1,500 activists have been killed since Mendes in 1988, most in the same cruel manner, with few antagonists brought to justice.

What now? The future of Earth's largest rainforest, the planet's two million square mile lungs, hangs in the balance and, along with it, our global climate. On a high note, international uproar has forced the Brazilian government to slow deforestation and work to halt it altogether by 2030. A proposed dam was scrapped, and behemoth corporations from beef to shoes to high-end handbags have boycotted materials sourced from razed forestland. More than eight million acres of the Amazon are protected in extractive reserves, and, in some Brazilian states, deforestation has nearly come to a standstill.

It's a promising start but a tall order in a nation of economic turmoil, and recent reports show a backslide in prior progress. The threat is greater than ever and inaction will be catastrophic. Experts confirm we have 15 years, give or take, until there is little rainforest left to save. We can look the other way and let it happen, watch the environment's death throes, or learn from Chico and make a stand.

HIS LEGACY

"I have already escaped six attempts on my life . . . still I have a moral commitment to myself. I cannot abandon the struggle, even if one day I should be struck with an assassin's bullet."

Chico Mendes's blood was born and spilled in the rainforest. In the time between, he inspired Indigenous people in establishing the world's first tropical forest conservation initiative and helped create Brazil's extractive reserve areas, beginning with the 40,000-square-hectare Seringal Sao Luis de Remanso. On the heels of his murder came a handful of victories—a halt to subsidized logging and ranching, protection of rubber preserves, and creation of Nature reserves. Sustainability is now an accepted and viable alternative to indiscriminate deforestation, and large-scale financiers are more inclined to back sustainable operations.

Even headstrong cattle ranchers have taken notice, to a degree, of sustainability's importance and benefit as a viable economic asset.

In 1987, Mendes received the United Nations Environment Program (UNEP) Global 500 Award "for environmental activism in the face of immense social, political, and logistical obstacles" and the National Wildlife Federation's National Conservation Achievement Award a year later. His book, *Fight for the Forest: Chico Mendes in His Own Words*, was posthumously published in 1989.

No one has done as much as Chico to preserve what is left of the Amazon, but today's conservation crusaders carry on his legacy to help mitigate and, hopefully, stop a devastating outcome.

THE NEXT GENERATION
OF CLIMATE CRUSADERS

Courage is the resolve to do well without the assurance of a happy ending.

—KATE MARVEL

IN THE CAB OF GEM, THE WORLD'S LARGEST WALKING DRAGLINE excavator, George Washington Hayduke jams a lever forward engaging the beast's innards, points its filthy snout toward a steep cliff in the depths of a strip mine, and triumphantly drives off the edge, into oblivion, infamy, victory.

Emily Johnston journeyed halfway across the country to a tar-sands oil pipeline site at the Canada-Minnesota border, shimmied past a fence into one of those "keep out" places and flipped the emergency shut-off valve. Promptly arrested, Johnston defended her actions as a "necessity in response to a climate emergency."

Hayduke is Edward Abbey's fictional but revered *Monkey Wrench Gang* hero. Johnston is the real-life herald of a frustrated and overwhelmed generation forced to live on a wounded planet, and, in some cases, adopt a conviction of radical environmentalism similar to what Abbey's story inspired nearly a half-century ago.

Much of the angst derives from a place of hopelessness. Scientists in the late 1980s warned the US government that climate change (they called it global warming back then) was already happening. Virtually nothing significant was done to address the issue. Earth's CO_2 levels today are at their highest concentrations in human history, far beyond what is considered suitable for human life. It is mind-boggling that this is happening, that we have pillaged to the point of endangering our own existence.

Early environmentalists joined "save the planet" rallies in a time of free thinking and revolution against the mainstream; today's younger generation rises from desperation—their future hangs in the balance and the only way to make a difference is to change the storyline. We need alternatives to the status quo reality: new possibilities to break people out of the trance of incremental change and trendy green initiatives that look good on the surface but do little to alter the habits of a consumptive society.

"Resist much. Obey little." Walt Whitman's simple but effective prescription rings true with the next generation of conservation crusaders. Here is a look at just a few of the names from around the world driving change today, to garner hope for tomorrow.

ISRA HIRSI, MINNEAPOLIS, MINNESOTA

"If we don't stop the climate crisis soon, those already impacted will be hit even more and generations like mine won't have a livable future." Isra Hirsi joined an environmental club in high school and went on to cofound and help direct the US Youth Climate Strike to educate voters on presidential candidates' positions on climate change. She continues to lobby Minneapolis to reach 100 percent renewable electricity by 2030 "because it shouldn't be whether it's politically possible, but what is necessary."

JAMIE MARGOLIN, SEATTLE, WASHINGTON

"Life as we know it is coming to an end thanks to climate change and rapid environmental destruction." Margolin is cofounder and co–executive director of Zero Hour, dedicated to giving Generation Z a climate change voice. "How am I supposed to plan and care about my future when my leaders aren't doing the same?" The fiercely driven Margolin believes addressing climate change requires "dismantling all the systems of oppression that caused it in the first place."

GRETA THUNBERG, SWEDEN

Thunberg became an overnight household name with her 2018 speech at the United Nations Climate Change Conference and school day strikes. Her very public action inspired millions of students around the world and launched the "Greta effect." "Since our leaders are behaving like children, we will have to take the responsibility they should have taken long ago." Thunberg's admirable efforts earned a Nobel Peace Prize nomination, and she has since led other school strikes and has spoken at COP25 in Chile and the UN Climate Summit. "We have to understand what the

LIONEL BONAVENTURE/CONTRIBUTOR/AFP/©GETTY IMAGES

older generation has dealt to us, what mess they have created that we have to clean up and live with. We have to make our voices heard."

AUTUMN PELTIER, CANADA

At age 13, Autumn Peltier addressed UN General Assembly leaders on critical water protection issues and later gained international attention in confronting Canadian prime minister Justin Trudeau on his lackadaisical water protection efforts and support for oil pipelines. Peltier is globally known as the "water warrior" and chief water commissioner of the Anishinabek Nation. Her work has inspired Indigenous youth and others around the world to make responsible water use decisions.

ALEXANDRIA VILLASEÑOR, NEW YORK

Alexandria Villaseñor remembers visiting Davis, California, in the midst of statewide wildfires and seeing people collapsing in the street from smoke inhalation. Learning that climate change is heavily influencing ravaging fires, Villaseñor started Earth Uprising, an innovative nonprofit organizing action and educating through scientist-written curriculum distributed by students to teachers. The program's mission statement says it all: "Earth Uprising isn't an organization. It's a battle cry. We are young people across the world who won't stay silent while our future is destroyed."

XIUHTEZCATL MARTINEZ, COLORADO

Xiuhtezcatl Martinez gave his first public speech at age 6, urging parents to teach their kids about Earth's sacred place in our lives. By age 15 he took part in a lawsuit against the government's failure to curb emissions, thus trampling children's rights. He has been part of President Obama's Youth Council and formally addressed the United Nations. As youth director for Earth Guardians, Martinez engages with young people to inspire effective leadership in conservation arenas. "That allowed me to engage in a conversation much bigger than myself. It's been something that has given me a lot of hope."

KALLAN BENSON, MARYLAND

"Don't be intimidated by what you think you can't do. Do what you can. Learn about the issue. It's important to focus on making better choices and decisions, not on finding the 'right' solution or answer." National coordinator for Fridays for Future USA and co-organizer of the Outreach Working Group for Fridays for Future International, Kallan Benson's efforts have galvanized an active, collaborative environmental movement. Her group helps organize nearly 140 community strikes in communities across the country and in her spare time she codirects Parachutes for the Planet, an art museum initiative encouraging participants to express their concerns for the future through community art. Her activism sparked a statewide fracking ban in Maryland and similar bills to reduce fossil fuel dependence.

JEROME FOSTER II, WASHINGTON, DC

How's this for a list of achievements? By age 16, Jerome Foster II was a Smithsonian Ambassador, founder and editor-in-chief of the *Climate Reporter*, and had received a D.C. State Board of Education Leadership and Commitment Award, Union of Concerned Scientists' Defender of Science Award, and an Audubon Naturalist Society 2020 Youth Environmental Champion Award, to name but a few. He also hosted youth climate strikes at the White House during the global strike movement and founded OneMillionOfUs, an organization promoting youth voting and advocacy. "Adults take note of this message: Young people like myself should not have to take on this burden, this is supposed to be your job but now we have to go on hunger strikes, meet with government officials, and start a global movement for you to even notice."

EYAL WEINTRAUB, ARGENTINA

"We have reached a point in history when we have the technical capacities to solve poverty, malnutrition, inequality and of course global warming. The deciding factors for whether we take advantage of our potential will be our activism and our international unity." At 18, Eyal Weintraub teamed with fellow activist Bruno Rodriguez in organizing a protest at the Buenos Aires national congress. He is active with a youth climate activist group called Jovenes Por El Clima and fights to inspire consistent, targeted activism to make a difference with climate change.

SAOI O'CONNOR, IRELAND

Since age 4, Saoi O'Connor showed a streak of dissent working with her parents on their Fair-Trade Committee. She grew up to be one of Ireland's brightest firebrands of the country's youth climate rebellion. "If a politician comes to my door, I start asking them hard questions. Some of them are shocked. . . . The politicians we elect have a direct influence over whether or not my generation inherits a livable planet." The "Irish Greta Thunberg" is active in the Fridays for Future protest movement.

INSPIRATION WITHIN

IN THE PANTHEON OF NATURE WRITING—BE IT DEEP-THINKING philosophy, reflective observation, or battle cry—the names in this book are among the greats. Even better, they prolifically penned their thoughts on the pages of dozens of books available far and wide to stir your outdoors-infused inclinations. Some of these titles are perfect for sparking philosophical debate with like-minded brethren, while others inspire sentiment of that place close to your heart or the one you want to visit. And a few are must-haves in a backpack with a week of wilderness in front of you. I recommend reading every one on this list and their compatriots. My personal favorites? Leopold for his persistence in driving change, Muir's exuberance and legendary achievements, Olson for what he saved in Minnesota's North Country, Carson's tenacity, and Abbey's dry wit mixed with a penchant to stop and savor it.

Enjoy.

Henry David Thoreau
Walden
Walking
The Maine Woods
Faith in a Seed

Aldo Leopold
A Sand County Almanac
Round River
For the Health of the Land

John Muir
Travels in Alaska
My First Summer in the Sierra
The Wilderness World of John Muir

Sigurd Olson
Listening Point
The Singing Wilderness
Reflections from the North Country
Of Time and Place

Rachel Carson
Silent Spring
The Sea Around Us
The Edge of the Sea
The Sense of Wonder

Edward Abbey
Desert Solitaire
The Monkey Wrench Gang
The Journey Home
A Voice Crying in the Wilderness
Slumgullion Stew
The Serpents of Paradise
Confessions of a Barbarian

Rosalie Edge
The Everglades, River of Grass

David Brower
Let the Mountains Talk

ENVIRONMENTAL MONUMENT TIMELINE

I MENTION SEVERAL NOTABLE MONUMENTS OF ENVIRONMENTAL history throughout this book, such as the signing of the Wilderness Act, establishment of the National Park Service, wildlife preservation efforts, and nationwide conservation movements. All had an enormous impact on the state of Nature in America and beyond. In our go-fast worlds, it's easy to overlook what came before and how it changed the landscape of our lives. Here's a look at some of Nature's big moments.

1872—Yellowstone becomes America's first national park.

1892—The Sierra Club is formed.

1933—The Civilian Conservation Corps is founded by FDR during the Great Depression, showing the value of organized activism.

1951—The Nature Conservancy is established. The venerable agency continues work protecting millions of acres of land around the world and spearheading dedicated conservation efforts.

1953—Jacques Cousteau's *Silent World* brings the fascinating underwater world to living rooms around the globe and sparks attention to sustainability.

1955—The Air Pollution Act passes Congress.

1956—The Sierra Club prevents the Echo Park Dam project from forever changing the Colorado River.

1962—*Silent Spring* is published.

1963—The Clean Air Act passes, paving the way for emissions regulations.

1965—The Water Quality Act passes, establishing federal water quality standards.

1968—Paul Ehrlich's *The Population Bomb* attributes environmental problems to overpopulation.

1968—The Wild and Scenic Rivers Act passes Congress.

1970—The National Environmental Policy Act passes Congress and America celebrates the first Earth Day.

1970—The Environmental Protection Agency is established.

1972—DDT is banned in the United States.

1973—The Endangered Species Act is passed.

1977—President Jimmy Carter pledges to reduce America's use of fossil fuels and move toward renewable energy.

1988—President Reagan signs the Ocean Dumping Ban Act.

1990—The Oil Pollution Act passes; the Indigenous Environmental Network is formed.

2015—A global climate change protocol is presented at the COP 21 summit; American youth file a climate change lawsuit against the federal government.

2019—Greta Thunberg ignites a global youth climate movement.

On the other side of the pendulum swing, here are just a few environmental setbacks over the years:

1969—A Santa Barbara oil well explosion spews more than 200,000 gallons of oil into the ocean. That same year, chemicals floating on Ohio's Cuyahoga River burst into flames.

Early 1980s—The world's population balloons to 4.5 billion with virtually no positive change in environmental issues.

1986—The Chernobyl nuclear power plant in Ukraine explodes, killing thirty-one people and depositing radioactive material to many European regions.

1989—Just one of thousands of oil spills, an Exxon oil tanker runs aground in Prince William Sound, Alaska, spilling eleven million gallons.

2008—A Tennessee coal plant accident unloads more than a billion gallons of coal fly ash sludge from a holding dam.

2010—The Deepwater Horizon oil drilling platform off the Louisiana coast explodes, killing eleven people and dumping millions of gallons of oil into the Gulf of Mexico.

2016–2020—Nearly one hundred environmental policies were reversed during the Trump Administration. Restrictions on power plant emissions were lifted, more than half of America's wetlands were no longer protected, the Clean Power Plan and industrial polluters were deregulated, and more than nine million acres of Alaska's Tongass National Forest were removed from roadless protection.

Also under threat is the Arctic National Wildlife Refuge to oil and gas extraction, the Migratory Bird Treaty Act, National Environmental Policy Act, Endangered Species Act rules, and clean water and air regulations.

To date, Americans' carbon budgets are at around 20 tons per year, compared to European countries at 10 tons and some developing nations at only 1 ton.

AN OPEN INVITATION

WRITING THIS BOOK WAS A FASCINATING JOURNEY. EVERY CHAPter brought learning, wonder, fulfillment, some laughs, and, most of all, inspiration. How about you? My sincere hope is you enjoyed the stories here and that these closing pages fill you with energy to become your own thinker, doer, or fighter. Perhaps that means marching to your local government in support of a place or cause. Maybe this is a time for volunteering your skills, diving into learning more about a new component of Nature, or reading an armload of books by authors past and present.

Whatever inspires you, I'll give you a head start with a list of popular, respected, or otherwise proven organizations making a difference. Be sure to check groups in your home area as well. Have a look around, find something that moves you, and go do great things. We have one planet, one home, and it's in trouble. But we can drive change by taking action. Let's write a new chapter to our story.

Think. Do. Fight.

The Nature Conservancy	nature.org
Sierra Club	sierraclub.org
National Audubon Society	audubon.org
World Wildlife Fund	worldwildlife.org
Rainforest Alliance	rainforest-alliance.org
Friends of the Earth	foe.org

Worldwatch Institute — climatenetwork.org
Leonardo DiCaprio Foundation — leonardodicaprio.org
League of Conservation Voters — lcv.org
National Parks Conservation Association — npca.org

Earth Island Institute — earthisland.org
Ocean Conservancy — oceanconservancy.org
Oceana — oceana.org
National Geographic Society — nationalgeographic.org
Climate Action Network — climateaction.org
The Wilderness Society — wilderness.org
Center for Biological Diversity — biologicaldiversity.org
Rocky Mountain Institute — rmi.org
Coral Reef Alliance — coral.org
Environmental Defense Fund — edf.org
Trust For Public Land — tpl.org

ABOUT THE AUTHOR

Steve Johnson is a self-propelled recreation junkie and fan of all things outdoors. Author of more than twenty outdoor interest titles and regular contributor to award-winning magazines across the country, he also partners with some of America's most influential business leaders to write their riveting stories, including an in-progress look at sustainability efforts around the world. Steve's lifelong passion for Nature inspired responsible outdoor recreation efforts in the Upper Midwest and Colorado, as well as student-led conservation campaigns including Small Grass Big Earth, a movement to reclaim millions of acres of America's lawns. Steve hails from Wisconsin's far north.